TRAGIC
MEANINGS
IN
SHAKESPEARE

Studies in
Language and
Literature

TRAGIC
MEANINGS
IN
SHAKESPEARE

Thomas McFarland
The City University of New York

RANDOM HOUSE · NEW YORK

for
Robert Crawford

Acknowledgments

The dedication expresses, inadequately, my gratitude for invaluable encouragement that I received in the actual conception and writing of this book. I wish also to acknowledge the assistance, and salute the memory, of four people who died before the work was commissioned or planned, but without whose interest it could never have come to be. To Theodore Spencer of Harvard University I owe my introduction to the serious and humane study of Shakespeare. To Myron Williams of The Phillips Exeter Academy I am indebted for kindness during early discouragements. I received my first and most important help from my father and mother, Thomas Alfred McFarland and Lucile Sylvester McFarland. Especially at this time do I think of my mother, whose courage and devotion, after the death of my father, made my education possible.

Thomas McFarland

Contents

TRAGIC
MEANINGS
IN
SHAKESPEARE

The Meaning of
Tragedy

Tragedy is the mirror of human existence. From our position amid the varied events of daily life, just as from our eyes looking out on the world, we can see much, but not our own selves. To see the events of the world, we look at the world; but to see ourselves, we need a mirror.

We look into the tragic mirror, however, not only to view our full reality, but also to set at a remove its rending paradox. Part of the truth of our existence is that nothingness bounds us on all sides; we came crying hither, and we all go into the dark. Yet madness looms if we look too long at our own deaths. "Human kind," as Eliot says, "cannot bear very much reality." Though we all grow old and die, for that very reason we find it wise to look only glancingly at such certain futurity. "Is not the fear of death natural to man?," asks Boswell, and Johnson replies: "So much so, Sir, that the whole of life is but keeping away the thought of it."

The tragic mirror is, therefore, a shield of Perseus by whose artifice we look on what would otherwise freeze and congeal our sight. "If in real life," says Cassirer, "we had to endure all those emotions through which we live in Sophocles's *Oedipus* or in Shakespeare's *King Lear* we should scarcely survive the shock and strain. But art turns all these pains and outrages, these cruelties and atrocities, into a means of self-liberation." If we were caught in a shipwrecking storm at sea, our sense of form and meaning would be inundated in the fearfulness of the event; but if we read of a storm at sea, we can increase, rather than lessen, our sense of security thereby. "Man's nature cannot carry/ Th' affliction nor the fear," says a Kent—but the affliction and fear inside the world of *King Lear* render us, in our lives outside that world, somehow unafflicted and unafraid.

For a mirror image is a reversed truth. Children see dramatic depictions of monsters, and their security on their playroom couch can be enhanced by these very horrors that, outside the mirror, would turn them to stone. Widows read murder mysteries far into the night, and the anxiety of the night is thereby dispelled. Aristotle's "catharsis" and Nietzsche's "metaphysische Trost" (metaphysical consolation), though differing in emphasis as conceptions of tragedy's function, both recognize this reversing effect of art.

But the mirror of existence not only shows us the form of emotion while freeing us from the consequence and responsibility of situation; it also shows us ourselves in a wholeness that we cannot attain from any point in our daily lives. Our daily lives are fragmented. We dwell on a hope of the morrow, or sting with a defeat from yesterday; much of our time we dissipate in inauthentic modes of meaningless chatter, careless curiosity, or indistinct cognizance—we sleep, we are bored, we are buried under repetitions. Only as children is our trip to the city a vivid and filled experience; as adults, the same trip, in its hundredfold repetitions, becomes lost in yesterday or three weeks ago.

Thus, the images in the mirror are, in a sense, more real than are we ourselves. More artificial, certainly, but no less existent; "the exhortation," Kenneth Burke once wittily wrote, "that the artist 'deal with life' is confusing, particularly as it is hard to understand how he could deal with anything else." Othello is as real as our five-years-ago-selves are real—that is, he exists as a symbolic phenomenon of our past. Hamlet is as real as Napoleon; neither exists except in our symbolic past, both exist in full orientation to a world. The present, on which we base all our claims to subsisting reality, flows from under us faster than thought—is, perhaps, merely a figment of memory and anticipation. King Lear is not only as real as our great-great-grandfathers, but more real—we know more by far of Lear than of those dim ancestors. The whole efficacy of art, whereby artifice does not imply diminished reality, depends on this fact of a universal democracy of existence, in which all events, regardless of their conventional emphasis, are simply, in the term of Descartes and Husserl, *cogitationes* (thoughts). Our art is as real as our history; our history as real as our hopes.

With such confidence in the dignity of its image, therefore, we look into the mirror of existence not only to see our lives reflected, but to see them focused. We look to see ourselves lifted, in our meaningful moments, from the dissipations and inauthenticities that erode our daily time.

But we cannot judge of meaning until we see the whole. As we would not tear out and attempt to judge a corner of a painting, so we cannot affirm or deny the worth of life without seeing the fullness of life. And the fullness of life—of any human life—is attained only at its extension to death. We feel the fact to be an absurdity, but we know it to be a truth: complete life cannot be separated from death. "Count no mortal happy," says the final chorus of *Oedipus Rex,* "till he has passed the final limit of his life secure from pain." And as for happiness, so for other meanings if we wish to speak of them with finality. Existence must be seen as a whole.

In death as mere event, however, tragedy has no interest. Death as isolated event is the end of meaning. "Der Tod ist kein Ereignis des Lebens," says Wittgenstein—"Den Tod erlebt man nicht": "death is no event of life"; "death is not experienced"—in the sense of being lived through. Only as the defining limit of life, and, therefore, as the affect of life, does the event of death appear in the mirror of existence.

But death is a symbol as well as an event. Death is an emblem—the most startling and therefore the most frequently employed—of a larger reality, that of non-being. Great tragedy—*Philoctetes,* or *Oedipus Rex*—has been composed without the death of the protagonist; but no tragedy can be conceived without the emphasized presence of non-being.

For where the event of death stands as a limit to our existence, non-being is a process; non-being invades, rather than awaits, our lives. Thus, Heidegger points out that death is with us every moment as a "being toward death"—*Sein zum Tode.* Our life is never free from non-being, whether in the form of age, sickness, catastrophe, or in the form of "absence, darknesse, death; things which are not."

The deepest paradox of existence resides in this fact —that non-being is both alien and integral to our lives. Our minds cannot work except by the simultaneous affirmation of being and non-being. To say that anything is, is to say that it is not—the law of identity and the law of contradiction are the same: if A is A, then A is not B; if John Smith is John Smith, he is not John Doe. If he is twenty-seven, he is not eighteen. If he is in America, he is not in Germany. It is, says Sartre, "the constant possibility of non-being, outside us and within us, that conditions the questions we can ask and the answers we can give to them."

Our very nature is a compound of being and non-being. We cannot step twice into the same river. The eyes that began to read this book are lost forever in the abysm of time. The youth grows pale, and spectre-thin, and dies. And if he lives, he does so only to grow old. When palsy shakes a few, sad, last gray hairs, the non-being of his youth will be bleakly apparent to him and others. "All creatures," says the great Leibniz, "derive from God and from nothingness. Their self-being is of God, their non-being is of nothing. . . . No creature can be without non-being; otherwise it would be God." "We have no claim to pure being," says Plutarch in a passage loved by Montaigne, "because all human nature is ever midway between being born and dying. . . . And if you chance to fix your thought on trying to grasp its essence, it would be neither more nor less than if you tried to clutch water." The youth of twenty-one is both twenty-one years into life and twenty-one years into death.

We look into the mirror of existence, accordingly, to try to separate our real from our impermanent—to try to extricate our being from nothingness. "The only self-knowledge," says Leibniz, "is to distinguish well between our self-being and our non-being." We seek ourselves in the mirror of existence.

And nothing other than ourselves is there to be found. Tragic drama does not communicate. It teaches us no new truths. It has no message. The artifice of the mirror is to reflect; what it reveals is only what we present to it. Men like Goethe or Coleridge revel in *Hamlet;* small men can find no meaning in its action.

Nor does the tragic mirror reflect for those who have not become aware of the non-being of existence. Children, who think they will live forever, are therefore depressed, rather than uplifted, by tragic art. A child of seven can see only chaos in *King Lear;* the pre-adolescent, only foolishness in *Antony and Cleopatra.*

Nor, again, do we look into the tragic mirror for pleasure. We read popular novels for relaxation; we read *Hamlet* for confirmation of our being. The view into the tragic mirror is an act of self-identification.

To see meaning in human life, despite the fact of our universal nothingness, is the task, demanding and exalting, of tragedy. But only because we are *Sein zum Tode* do we need the tragic mirror. It is not difficult, from the perspective of an angel infancy, vibrating with bright shoots of everlastingness, to see meaning in life; all problems are resolved by the confidence of immortality, by the belief that the future brings an accession of being, by the formula "and then they lived happily ever after." In this and other states in which we feel no threat of devouring time, the problem of meaning hardly arises. "The solution of the problem of life," says Wittgenstein, "is to be seen in the disappearance of this problem."

In his next breath, however, Wittgenstein honors the paradox of adulthood: "But is it possible for one so to live that life stops being problematic? That one is *living* in eternity and not in time? . . . Only a man who lives not in time but in the present is happy." And yet even golden lads and girls all must, as chimney-sweepers, come to dust. The mighty truth not known to the child —Wordsworth's "best philosopher"—is the truth of sad mortality. We are prepared for the sight of tragedy's mirror only when we realize that we live in war with time, and that the wrackful siege of battering days digs deep trenches in our happiness, confidence, and sense of meaning.

Human life is mortality. Shipwreck—"Scheitern"— is our universal lot. "We with the vessel of mortalitie fleing away," say Castiglione and Hoby, "go one after another through the tempestuous sea, that swalloweth up and devoureth all thinges, neither is it graunted us at any time to come on shore againe, but alwaies beaten with contrarie windes, at the ende wee breake our vessell at some rocke." With the aid of illusions—either gross or sophisticated—we can affirm easy meanings for life; but securities found in illusion are illusion themselves. The index of tragedy's dignity is that of its difficulty: to look steadily and whole at the terror of life and nonetheless find meaning. This meaning is not meaning of translatability, but meaning of unshakable conviction. When the sun is out, we know it to be out, and not all the logic of the school can sway our knowledge. The certainty of truth, as Spinoza said, lights both itself and error.

The paradoxicality of tragedy (that we see the highest meaning of life only as we see the full fact of mortality) combines with the untranslatability of its meaning (like the response to great music) to point toward the truth enunciated by Jaspers: "There is no tragedy without transcendence." At the very moment in which we realize that the individual—Nietzsche's *principium individuationis*—must inevitably be swallowed up in the blank and primordial Dionysian oneness—at that very moment emerges the sense of transcendence: the sense of something more. And this something more, rising out of the spectacle of man's defeat by non-being, is the meaning of tragedy. It is meaning untranslatable, but meaning unmistakable. It is a "heavenly quintessence," a radiant song from our chains, the swan-song of anticipation heard by Socrates. Such is the nature, evanescent and transcendent, of the realm behind the images in the tragic mirror.

But we sight that realm only in the mirror. The "pools of non-being"—in Sartre's phrase—that we encounter in daily life may dampen our spirits or even drown us; but they are too roiled to reveal us to ourselves. Tragic transcendence is meaning achieved only through human artifice. The crash of an airplane is a catastrophic happening; yet only if it were reflected in art could it be seen as a tragic event. For only by an act of reflection do we glimpse the transcendent dimensions of our existence.

The transcendences of *King Lear* and *Antony and Cleopatra* are the brightest that tragic art has achieved; but *Hamlet,* which seems to deny that life has meaning, possesses its own obverse splendor. "The truth once seen," says Nietzsche,

> man is aware everywhere of the ghastly absurdity of existence. . . . Dionysiac man might be said to resemble Hamlet: both have looked deeply into the true nature of things, they have *understood* and are now loath to act. They realize that no action of theirs can work any change in the eternal condition of things. . . . Understanding kills action, for in order to act we require the veil of illusion.

But the heart that cracks in Hamlet is a noble heart, and in the modification "noble," earned by the process of the play, resides the transcendence of *Hamlet*. Though the prince goes down to the dark, we, if, for our part, *we* have understood, know that he is more, not less, than when the play began.

In its rising, out of the recognition of disharmony, defeat, and nothingness, to a transcendent affirmation, tragedy parallels the movement of Christianity. Indeed, as Coleridge realized, all great art moves in the sphere of religion. And though Jaspers denies that tragedy and Christianity are commensurate—though others, from other perspectives, have agreed in his denial (Clifford Leech, for instance, or Laurence Michel)—the continuing need to reject the identity of the two realms functions as a witness to their similarity.

Yet it is true that tragedy and Christianity are not

interchangeable. One is image, the other reality; one distills meaning from this world, the other has faith in the next. Christianity and tragedy, as twin rails for existence's car, though parallel in our temporal concern, can thereby never meet; and the final face to face that will supersede all partial knowledge is beyond the possibility of tragedy. But all great tragedy points us out of our bondage. In this world, in our existential chains, tragedy and Christianity share the same longing for that which is beyond our reality—ἐπέκεινα τῆς οὐσίας.

The groundwork not only of tragic drama but of religion is the disruption between what our reason tells us and what our hearts desire. Our spirits do not fit this world; a stone is solely a stone, but mortals are not content with mortality. Our certain knowledge of what the future will bring ("Luck's a chance, but trouble's sure") is always contradicted by hope that "all these woes" of existence "shall serve/ For sweet discourses in our times to come." The "tragic combat," says Unamuno, the "very essence of tragedy," is the "combat of life with reason." The "spirit of unsubmissiveness to death labours to build up the house of life," while "the keen blasts and stormy assaults of reason beat it down." The "vital longing for human immortality finds no consolation in reason . . . and reason leaves us without incentive or consolation in life and life itself without real finality." Thus it is that "the discovery of death is that which reveals God to us"; for "be it with reason or without reason, or against reason, I am resolved not to die." But this craving for what we are not, this wish to exchange the non-being of mortality for the being of immortality, is the most inexplicable phenomenon of man. "No rational man," says Dr. Johnson, "can die without uneasy apprehension. . . . Few believe it certain they are . . . to die; and those who do, set themselves to behave with resolution, as a man does who is going to be hanged.

He is not the less unwilling to be hanged." Tragedy and religion have a common ground in the disjunction between our knowledge of the universality of death, and our sense of the wrongness of such a future.

If tragedy and religion thus share a common involvement, so too do tragedy and philosophy. "To be a philosopher is to learn to die," muses Montaigne. "True philosophers," says Socrates, "make dying their profession" (*Phaedo* 67E). "Those who really apply themselves to philosophy in the right way are always preparing themselves for dying and death" (*Phaedo* 64A). And Unamuno urges the paradox that though philosophy and religion are enemies, nonetheless the "history of philosophy is, strictly speaking, a history of religion."

The common term of such equations is the tragic tension between our knowledge of non-being and our need for being—a tension that exists in both philosophy and religion regardless of whether these realms of concern are overtly linked or deliberately separated. Thus, on the one hand, Descartes, in surveying human incompleteness, imperfection, and non-being, finds such phenomena the benchmark impressed by the Creator on his work—hence to us, a reminder of God. Sartre, on the other hand, interprets our incompleteness and non-being in an atheistic framework. The being toward which human reality transcends itself is thereby "not a transcendent God," but merely "itself as totality." And yet Sartre, like Descartes, acknowledges the fact central to tragedy, that "l'être imparfait se dépasse vers l'être parfait; l'être qui n'est fondement que de son néant se dépasse vers l'être qui est fondement de son être"—"the imperfect being, man, passes beyond itself toward the perfect being; the being that is the foundation only of its nothingness transcends toward the being that is the foundation of its being." For tragedy, whether it look toward Christian finalities, or whether it be conceived as a strictly secular, even an atheistic, recognition of human placement, always witnesses the fact that human existence must seek horizons beyond its circumstances. Tragedy is an offering to the indestructibility and incommensurability of the human spirit.

Tragic meaning, therefore, underlies all our recognitions of the situation of man. That painting of Rembrandt's, where, against a dark background, an old but infinitely noble man wears a mysterious golden helmet, is an epitome of all tragic realization. The helmet, gleaming, pointing upward, both symbolizes the mystery of the human mind and points toward the transcendent origin of all our light, while the bearded and hoary countenance beneath the helmet shadows forth our universal destiny of death. The sadness of the face links with the darkness against which it stands; the dignity of the face links with the mysterious artifice of the helmet.

Not even a Rembrandt, however, not even a Socrates, can express the range of tragic meanings possible to drama. For tragic drama alone portrays the *process* of life. Philosophy, religion, painting, deal with propositions, conceptions, objects—but tragic drama portrays human beings moving in time, and only as movement in time does human existence attain its full dimension.

Thus, Heidegger emphasizes that *Sorge*—care, concern, involvement—is the essence of existence. But *Sorge* is a "structure" that needs time for its fullness. We care not only for what lies about us ("Sein-bei [innerweltlich begegnendem Seienden]"), but for what already has been and may be about to happen ("Sich-vorweg-schon-sein-in [einer Welt]")—and the latter formula indicates events that actually are *a part of* the encounters signalized by the former. Hence, as Heidegger realizes, present, past, and future are not real divisions of time, but modes of existence. As *"Ekstasen der Zeitlichkeit"* they are all inseparable in any moment of existence, all necessary to the "Seinsganzheit des Daseins als Sorge"—"the total being of existence as care." But if the unity of the care-structure lies in the phenomenon of time ("Die . . . Einheit der Sorgestruktur liegt in der Zeitlichkeit"), care itself is thereby mixed with non-being ("Die Sorge selbst ist in ihrem Wesen durch und durch von Nichtigkeit durchsetzt"), and is a being toward death ("Die Sorge ist Sein zum Tode"). Existence, involvement, time, non-being, and being toward death are thus revealed, in Heidegger's phenomenological analysis, as necessarily intertwined. The deepest possibilities of tragic meaning, in other words, can be realized only by the consideration of concerns represented with reference to present, past, and future—by the consideration, that is, of the movement of human life in time.

Such an implication of existential analysis not only points to tragic drama as the most complete possibility for the extrication of meaning from non-being, but implies certain emphases in our present task, which is the critical interpretation of Shakespeare's greatest tragic achievement. Tragic drama shows human existence as concern in time. But the most important human meanings, we all know, arise only in our relations with our fellows. As Buber says, all true life is the encounter with other human beings ("alles wirkliche Leben ist Begegnung"). Only the interpretation, accordingly, that honors tragic drama not only as the concerns, but also as the encounters, of human existence can hope to reveal tragic meaning.

Now such an insistence both does and does not urge a return to the character explications that formed the basis of Coleridge's—and Bradley's—Shakespearean criticism. It does urge that image-counting, metaphorical analysis, linguistic or textual approaches, can never be more than preliminaries to meaning. It urges that all tragic meaning depends on the *as if* assumption that dramatic creations are human beings. Such is the underlying truth of the attitude represented by Coleridge and Bradley, and to that truth we must return.

We should not, however, return to old mistakes and methodological chaos. The distinctions developed by the phenomenological analysis of existence can protect the explication of character from the random psychologizing that was the weakness of the Coleridge–Bradley approach. By utilizing the safeguards supplied by the phenomenological approach, therefore, the interpreter can reaffirm the critical truth that only through character analysis is tragic meaning recovered, while at the same time he will not go astray in such futilities as the attempt—in the humorous rubric of L. C. Knights—to determine how many children had Lady Macbeth.

Of the nature of the phenomenological approach little need here be said. In the moments of its appearance in the following chapters, the method will seem—except to eyes familiar with the logical clarifications of Brentano and Husserl—almost indistinguishable from the method of New Criticism. Indeed, as Heidegger notes, "phenomenology" can be formulated as merely an exhortation to direct our attention to matters at hand ("zu den Sachen selbst!"). Or we may say, with Merleau-Ponty, that the phenomenological approach simply "tries to give a direct description of our experience as it is." The attempt neither adds to nor subtracts from our experience, but is rather a way of viewing it with certain shifts of emphasis and a certain refinement of our ordinary notions of relevance. The practical application of phenomenology, therefore, despite the complexity of the subject from a purely theoretical standpoint, does not require explanation in order to be clearly understood.

Moreover, the interpretations in this volume do not derive from the study of phenomenology; they take their origin, rather, solely in reflection on the statement and implication of the plays themselves. The phenomenological approach is here no more than a device for regulation and presentation, and as such is utilized frequently in the chapter on *Hamlet,* occasionally in the chapters on *Lear* and *Othello,* not at all in the chapter on *Antony and Cleopatra.* By the same token, although these interpretations sometimes appeal to the language and special distinctions of existence philosophy, they do so only for illustration or extension of their arguments. The arguments themselves do not grow out of, and do not depend upon, existence philosophy.

Nonetheless, the fact of their congeniality to the language of existence philosophy explicitly rejects the contention of much modern criticism—based originally on the viewpoints of Stoll, Wilson Knight, Knights and others—that Shakespeare's tragedies are to be understood primarily as linguistic or metaphoric structures rather than as representations of human character. These plays, on the contrary, are precisely "Sorgestrukturen." The meaning of tragic drama is inseparable from its nature as "Duwelt"—the human realm—and the abandonment of character explication, no matter how gross the critical abuses that urge such abandonment, perverts tragic action into formulations of "Eswelt"— the realm of thing.

So we look now into the four tragic mirrors that reveal life most fully and focus it most meaningfully. When we think of these plays as the achievement of a single mind, we are overcome by a fourfold wonder that we experience again only in the study of the *Phaedo, Phaedrus, Symposium,* and *Republic,* and in the contemplation of Mozart's four great operas. Yet not even those works display dimensions so vast, and the strength to support meanings so high, as do the tragedies of Shakespeare. For these plays seem almost the foursquare foundation for a New Jerusalem of the spirit.

Hamlet and the Dimension
of Possible Existence

Hamlet is a play that emphasizes the mystery of existence by illuminating the nature of human responsibility; and it sees this responsibility as a reflex of the phenomenon of human decision. The truism of popular oversimplification, that *Hamlet* is a play about a man who cannot make up his mind, attains, when restated in a context of existential awareness, the transparency of universal truth. The fact developed by Mack, and subsequently by Levin, that the language of the play is dominated by the interrogative mode, witnesses the importance of decision for the structure of its plot: every decision that I *will* do something always is yoked to an antecedent interrogation: *shall* I do it? And this question in its turn implies a still more abstract subjunction of concern: *ought* I to do it? There are, insists Kant in his first *Kritik,* three "questions" that combine "all the interests of my reason": "1. What can I know? 2. What ought I to do? 3. What may I hope?" The play of

Hamlet, by addressing itself to the second of these ultimate questions, encounters, in the implications of its
responses, the paradoxes that lie at the boundary of
human meaning.

The focusing question of *Hamlet,* "What ought I to
do?" has, however, been formulated extrinsically by
generations of critics as the question of delay: "Why
does Hamlet take so long to kill Claudius?" In some
anonymous remarks on the play, printed in London in
1736 and usually attributed to Hanmer, a bluntly practical answer is given: "Had Hamlet gone naturally to
work, as we could suppose such a prince to do in
parallel circumstances, there would have been an end to
our play." The combination of the sufficiency of this
answer on purely positivistic grounds and of its radical
insufficiency in terms of the seriousness of tragic discourse reveals to us the inadequacy of mere common
sense for the inspection of Shakespeare's tragic meaning.
Hamlet's deep involvement with events of possibility
points us, rather, toward a confrontation of its significance from the existential standpoint that emerges to our
view out of the paradoxes surrounding time.

Now the present, as Leibniz says, "est chargé du
passé, et gros de l'avenir"—filled with the past and great
with the future. The question first asked by the critic,
"Why does Hamlet take so long to kill Claudius?" for
its very asking involves the futurity of Hamlet's pro-
posed action and the pastness of the reasons for demanding the death of Claudius. And it thereby thrusts toward
a realization that the agency of Hamlet, which is the
subject of the question, incorporates, to a degree apparent in no other Shakespearean tragedy, that deepest
dimension of being ourselves that Jaspers calls
"mögliche Existenz"—possible existence. "Mögliche
Existenz" is the mode of understanding in which each of
us realizes that he is not merely a being limited by a set
of external facts at a given moment—a *Dasein*—but

rather the mysterious inward unity—an *Existenz*—that can say "my" or "mine" to separate events strung out in time: "my" childhood, "my" three-and-twentieth year, "my" thirtieth year to heaven, "my" death.

From the perspective of such a conception, the initial question, "Why does Hamlet take so long to kill Claudius?" becomes extrinsic to the play—is revealed as the question of a spectator. The question, as it arises existentially from within the play, is rather *"ought* I— and the choice is my choice—to kill Claudius?" For the *petitio principii* of Hanmer's extrinsic interpretation that Hamlet cannot kill Claudius because such an action would end the play, we substitute, from the intrinsic existential perspective, an equally practical, but far more satisfying solution: Hamlet does not kill Claudius because Hamlet has not made up his mind. Between the ghost's desire for revenge, and the consummation of that revenge, there stands the activity of an agent. But this agent is a being with choices and possibilities in the flow of time—a deciding *Existenz*—not a thing that may be activated by words as a machine is activated by levers. The fact that Claudius is not yet killed is inseparably entwined with the fact that he may, possibly, not be killed at all. It is possible that Hamlet will kill Claudius; but this possibility reveals the existential mystery of human freedom, for the possibility that Hamlet will kill Claudius is the very possibility that he will not kill Claudius. Hamlet must decide to kill Claudius, or he must decide not to kill Claudius.

If the posing of the question, "Ought I to kill Claudius?" implies the decision, the freedom, the possibility, and the responsibility of killing or not killing Claudius, it likewise implies time past and time future— both of which share a common existential form as "then." The "nows" realized by the presented action of the play of *Hamlet* are wrought upon constantly by portentous "thens." Hamlet is "now" called upon to kill

Claudius—in the play—because "then"—outside the play—Claudius killed Hamlet's father. Hamlet is "now" angry with Claudius's wife, because "then" she was his father's wife. Hamlet is "now" disillusioned by Rosencrantz and Guildenstern because "then" they were his friends. Denmark is "now" at odds with Norway, because "then" the now-dead Hamlet and the now-dead Fortinbras were in competition. "Why wouldst thou be a breeder of sinners?" queries Hamlet of Ophelia, his anger of the "now" spilling forward into a hypothetical "then" (III.i.122–3).* "I did love you once," says Hamlet, looking from the anguish of a "now" to a "then" of the past (III.i.116). "Alas, poor Yorick! I knew him, Horatio," says Hamlet, the "now" of the skull involving the mysterious "then" of twenty-three years ago (V.i.202–3). "It is not, nor it cannot come to good," says Hamlet of the present "now" and future "then" of his mother's remarriage (I.ii.158).

And the participation of the "now" in its temporal extensions as "then," as we see upon reflection, becomes also the participation of a logical "then" in its "if" premises. The antecedents of Hamlet's actions in time are their antecedents in causality also. "Because" Hamlet's father has been killed in past time, "then" Hamlet's future is mortgaged to the existence of Claudius. The hidden "then" of futurity in the question, "Ought I to kill Claudius?" transforms itself into a statement of special condition: "If I kill Claudius, what then?"

So uniquely, in fact, does this play illuminate the bondage of "now" to linkages, past and future, logical as well as temporal, of "then," that the articulations of the drama, as presented, and taken without these existential linkages, seem constantly either impoverished or para-

* All quotations from Shakespeare are taken from *The Complete Plays and Poems of William Shakespeare,* edited by William A. Neilson and Charles J. Hill, Houghton Mifflin Company, 1942.

doxical. Thus it is that T. S. Eliot complains that *Hamlet* lacks "objective correlatives"—correspondences in the concrete presentations of the play for the emotional intensity and emotional logic of its unfolding of character. We applaud the insight at the same time that we reject Eliot's conclusion that the play is thereby a failure. We realize, rather, that the hiddenness of *Hamlet* is the mark of its grandeur. This play, in a manner unique in Shakespeare's achievement, involves the past as reason for the present, the future as reason for the past, the present as arena for both past and future. In this play the "things that are made" depend for their full meaning, as they do in Christianity, upon the "invisible things" inferentially real, but not presented to our gaze.

One entire order of such invisible things is constituted by a repeated "otherness" in the indication of physical realm. Where *Antony and Cleopatra* changes its locale from Egypt to Italy to Sicily to Greece to Asia Minor, and attains thereby a resplendently expanded sense of spiritual landscape, the action of *Hamlet* is restricted to a small and straitened spot in Denmark. "Denmark's a prison" (II.ii.249) for the physical as well as the psychological situation of the drama. Indeed, the wonderful opening scene on the battlements of Elsinore locates us in a small corner of darkness and stone and huddled misery. Remarkably, however, this initial localization of presented action is torn at by constant reference to geographical places not presented. Characters are repeatedly either from, or toward, realms indicated as "elsewhereness," but not realized as scene. Hamlet is "from" Wittenberg, while Laertes is "toward" Paris. Rosencrantz and Guildenstern are "toward" England, while Claudius's ambassadors are "toward" Norway. Fortinbras is "from" Norway and "toward" Poland. Even Polonius, as his Latin name suggests, is, at some unspecified time, "from" Poland. But we do not see Wittenberg, and no scenes are laid in Paris; we never land in England, and the sledded Polacks are not glimpsed by our spectator eyes.

This motif of invisible geographic otherness constitutes a coordinate, in the space indications of the play, for the invisible "thens" of its time. The players are, in space, "from" some undefined area outside Denmark ("Com'st thou to beard me in Denmark?" asks Hamlet [II.ii.443]), but they are likewise, in time, from a "then" of former acquaintance with Hamlet ("By'r Lady, your ladyship is nearer to heaven than when I saw you last . . ." [II.ii.444–6]). Any "then"—such is the rule we discover—must be set in place as well as in time, must, in short, be a "then and elsewhere." And by the same token, any "now" is in fact a "here and now."

These emphases, realized in the phenomenological analysis of existence, provide us a key to the meaning of Hamlet's action. The agony of Hamlet erupts from the radical disjunction of the "here and now" of his situation in the play from the "then and elsewhere" of his possible existence. Hamlet remembers that Yorick "hath borne me on his back a thousand times." But this pleasure in the "then and elsewhere" is wrenchingly out of joint with the "here and now" of the skull:

> And now how abhorred in my imagination it is! . . .
> Here hung those lips that I have kiss'd I know not how
> oft. Where be your gibes now, your gambols, your
> songs, your flashes of merriment that were wont to set
> the tables on a roar? No one now, to mock your own
> grinning? Quite chapfall'n? Now get you to my lady's
> chamber, and tell her, let her paint an inch thick, to
> this favour she must come. Make her laugh at that.
>
> (V.i.205–15)

The wonderful anti-dialogue, by ringing changes on the motif of the death's head grin, grotesquely and startlingly epitomizes the play's persistent juxtaposition and disjunction of "then," "now," "here," and "elsewhere." By setting responsibilities into conflict, by forcing decision to the limits of the decidable, by disposing the meaning of characterization among the dead and past as well as the living and present, the play of *Hamlet* maps both the extent and limitation of possible existence, witnesses both the absurdity and propriety of man's conception of his dignity.

That dignity, not only in the play but in our life outside the play, depends on the paradox of an orientation toward a transcendent purpose and justification that, by its transcendence, continually eludes the present. Thus Jaspers affirms that "Existenz ist, was sich zu sich selbst und darin zu seiner Transzendenz verhält"—existence is that which in referring to itself refers to its transcendence—and that " 'Existenz' ist . . . kein Begriff, sondern Zeiger, der auf ein 'jenseits aller Gegenständlichkeit' weist"—existence is no concept, but a pointing to something beyond all factual presentness—and, climactically, "Dass sich Existenz nicht in sich schliesst, wird daher der Prüfstein aller Existenz-philosophie"—that the fact that existence cannot be contained in itself is the touchstone of all existence philosophy. The characters in the play of *Hamlet* are oriented, as are men in life, toward the world and its demands; but Hamlet, in special fullness of *Existenz,* is oriented as well toward absolute transcendence. Among the many "othernesses" from and toward which the action in *Hamlet* moves, the one most absolutely transcendent, and at the same time most pervasively and constantly indicated in the play's language, is that perfection of futurity that the Creed calls *vitam venturi saeculi,* and that we call heaven. As the "here and now" streams backward into the "then and elsewhere," and forward toward the "then and elsewhere," so Hamlet is "from" the sunlit humanism of Wittenberg, and "toward" the felicity of paradise.

In this omnipresent fact we see the use of the Christian matrix of the tragedy. In the most important source for Shakespeare's play, Belleforest's *Histoires tragiques,* the entire complex of law, morality, civilization, and— as symbol for all other transcendences, of religion— that we experience in *Hamlet* is markedly absent; instead, the action of the source story takes place in an explicitly non-Christian environment. Belleforest's tale begins (in the words of a translation printed in 1608) with the exhortation that

> You must understand, that long time before the kingdome of Denmark received the faith of Jesus Christ, and imbraced the doctrin of the Christians, that the common people in those dayes were barbarous and uncivill, and their princes cruel, without faith or loyaltie, seeking nothing but murther.

In Shakespeare's dramaturgy, however, this setting of unequivocal paganism is transformed into an equally insistent context of Christianity. When the dying Hamlet asks Horatio not to join him in death, the request is not to forgo a pagan suicide pact or a voyage to such a dim nether world as that inhabited by Homer's Patroclus, but to "Absent thee from felicity a while" (V.ii.358)—from the bliss of a Christian heaven. And the ironic possibility of alternate meaning, that perhaps even nothingness is felicity compared to "this harsh world," is rebuked by Horatio's Christian benediction, that "flights of angels sing thee to thy rest!" (V.ii.371). The assumption that reality is Christian, and divided into heaven and earth, is pervasive. The soldier Marcellus refers to the ghostly apparition in the context of "that season . . ./ Wherein our Saviour's birth is celebrated" (I.i.158–9). The conscience-stricken Claudius says that "my offence is rank, it smells to heaven;/ It hath the primal eldest curse upon't,/ A brother's murder." (III.iii.36–8); and he concludes by saying that "My words fly up, my thoughts remain below./ Words without thoughts never to heaven go" (III.iii.97–8). Hamlet refers to the Christian fact that "the Everlasting" has "fix'd/ His canon 'gainst self-slaughter!" (I.ii.131–2). The burial of Ophelia is a pointedly Christian event. And the word and thought of "heaven" are woven into the very texture of the play's language: "Would I had met my dearest foe in heaven" (I.ii.182); "With almost all the holy vows of heaven" (I.iii.114); "Leave her to heaven" (I.vi.86); "Heavens face doth glow" (III.iv.48); "Confess yourself to Heaven;/ Repent what's past" (III.iv.149–50). The cosmos of *Hamlet*, in short, is a world permeated by transcendence and the hope of heaven.

But the symbolic spiritual base—Wittenberg (where, in Marlowe's words, one "profits in divinity . . ./ In heavenly matters of theology")—the symbolic spiritual base that launches Luther on his career of heaven-seeking can also launch Dr. Faustus on an equally dynamic career of hell-finding. The irony of this double possibility accompanies Hamlet through all his strivings from his "then and elsewhere" spiritual origin toward his "then and elsewhere" spiritual goal of the future. Hamlet is a man walking with springy, confident steps along the pathway to the heavenly city, when suddenly the path forks, and the realization comes to him that now neither path leads to his goal. The tragedy of Hamlet is not attendant upon any incapacity on his part for decision, but upon a paradoxical boundary situation, an antinomy of knowledge itself. We must take stern exception to Goethe's conception that in this play "a lovely, pure and most moral nature, without the strength of nerve which forms a hero, sinks beneath a burden which it cannot bear and must not cast away." And we must likewise reject the view of Coleridge that Hamlet "knows well what he ought to do," that "he is full of purpose, but void of that quality of mind which accomplishes purpose." Nor can we accept Bradley's contention that it is "probable" that "Hamlet was not far from insanity," that "if we like to use the word 'disease' loosely, Hamlet's condition may truly be called diseased." On the contrary, it is not Hamlet's condition that is diseased, but his situation that is impossible. ("It is not madness/ That I have utt'red. Bring me to the test,/ And I the matter will re-word, which madness/ Would gambol from" [III.iv.141–4]). Hamlet, quite in opposition to the Romantic view that sees in him a delicate, introspective, withdrawing nature, is presented as a man who has "then and elsewhere" qualified himself in the eyes of his peers as "The expectancy and rose of the fair state,/ The glass of fashion and the mould of form,/ The observ'd of all observers" (III.i.160–2). His melancholy in the "here and now" is specifically referred to as a deviance from his expected bearing: "quite, quite down!" (III.i.162), says Ophelia, and Hamlet says, "I have of late . . . lost all my mirth"—implying that mirth is coordinate with his "custom of exercise" (II.ii.306–8).

Thus Hamlet's *ethos,* as Hartley Coleridge saw, is not that of a man who cannot arrive at a decision. The play posits, rather, a man proceeding through life with force and decision, with—until the "here and now" of the presented action—uninterrupted success: posits him, in short, as the beneficiary in a series of his own right decisions. If, as Ophelia says, Hamlet has become, in the stream of time, "the courtier's, soldier's, scholar's, eye, tongue, sword," he has, to that extent, decided for right dress as against wrong dress, for learning against ignorance, for skill in arms against ineptitude—and all such decisions for success, as we know from consulting our own lives, are the apex of a pyramid of innumerable supporting decisions. Hamlet is presented to us quite simply as a man accustomed to winning, a confident man, a man easy with his peers, admired by his subordinates. And even in the agony of his impossible choice, he makes decision after decision with confidence and alacrity. Not only does he stab the eavesdropper at the arras, but he consults with neither his mother nor himself before he does so. He displays no hesitation about hiding the body of Polonius and refusing to reveal its location. He shows neither hesitation nor scruple about hoisting Rosencrantz and Guildenstern with their own petard. There is no inactivity about his arranging the play-within-the-play. He is hindered by no delicate withdrawal of spirit in savagely attacking Ophelia, nor later, in leaping into her grave. He is afflicted by no inability to take a mental stand in his opinion about his mother's remarriage. Indeed, were we not almost hypnotized by the traditional view of his delicate and passive nature (Goethe's "köstliches Gefäss . . . das nur liebliche Blumen in seinen Schoss hättc aufnehmen sollen"— delicate vase . . . that should have received only lovely flowers), we would see that not only does Hamlet decide, and act, but he does so with bewildering rapidity and intensity.

But the one issue on which his ready decisiveness founders is the issue that makes the play: the command to kill Claudius.

Let us reflect upon what we all know: life is a constant series of decisions. Our daily existence is fragmented into innumerable questions, each pointing toward decision as the moment in which we discover the mysteriousness of our humanity. The waters that divide before the ship of life are the alternatives of decision. Indeed, as Kant emphasizes in the *Kritik der Urteilskraft,* it is the intellectual separation of possibility and actuality that distinguishes the human mind, as *intellectus ectypus,* from either animal or divine intelligence. "Shall I go to the play tonight?" we may ask, and by asking we suggest the futurity of our going tomorrow night, the pastness of our not having been last night, and the possibility of our not going at all. "Do I dare to eat a peach?" asks the little man, and his small question, in revealing to us that our existence unfolds in units of decision that may be almost infinitesimal in their import, likewise reveals to us that the topology of decision itself is time. If precisely at noon of a Tuesday I ask myself the question, "Do I dare to eat a peach?" the meaning of the question is inseparable from the premise that there will be a moment past noon in which either I will or will not so have dared.

But if the decision thrust upon Hamlet, to kill Claudius or not to kill Claudius, can, without lessening the necessity of its linkage of existence, possibility, responsibility, and time, be infinitesimally diminished to the Prufrockian peach-confrontation, likewise it can—and must—be expanded to the boundary situation of human existence taken as the continuum of possibilities. To kill or not to kill Claudius expands not only into the general question, to kill or not to kill a human being, but finally to the most general of all questions about human life confronted by the possibility of non-being: "To be or not to be, that is the question" (III.i.56). The famous words become a rubric that subsumes the entire "ought" focus of the play. "There is but one truly serious philosophical problem," says Camus in *Le Mythe de Sisyphe,* "and that is suicide. Judging whether life is or is not worth living amounts to answering the fundamental question of philosophy." "Why," asks Heidegger to begin his *Einführung in die Metaphysik,* "are there things that are, rather than nothing? This is the first of all questions, though not in a chronological sense." The question of Heidegger reveals, from a perspective lodged in abstract reason, precisely the same validating condition for possibility that the problem of Camus affirms from within the continuum of decision, and that the question, "To be or not to be," affirms for the dramatic situation of Hamlet.

To the command to kill Claudius, therefore, the deciding *Existenz* responds with the primary question, "Why?" In the Senecan revenge tradition from which the play of *Hamlet* departs, this question is customarily not asked, for in this tradition the answer is usually given beforehand. Tamora does not ask why she should avenge her son, nor does Titus ask why he should avenge his daughter. *The Revenger's Tragedy* opens with the protagonist—all questions of "why" already resolved by his very name, Vendice—holding up his mistress's skull and vowing revenge on her murderer. The interest of such a play consequently resides almost wholly in the details of the realization of the revenge. The play of *Hamlet,* on the contrary, by questioning the commandment to revenge, becomes not only the fulfillment of the Senecan revenge convention, but its abolition as well. In meditating on the differences between a Vendice and a Hamlet we are led to an appreciation of the wisdom of Aristotle's insistence that *mythos*—what we call plot—is more important for tragedy than *ethos,* or what we call character. For the *mythos* of Hamlet is not, as in *The Revenger's Tragedy,* melodramatic manipulation of event, but the existential unfolding of character in the matrix of time. Vendice is posited, as it were, as *Dasein* exclusively—character as a function of situation—while Hamlet is *Existenz* also—existence grounded in freedom, possibility, and responsibility. In his *ethos* Hamlet is, in a sense, ironically projected as an avatar of conflicting Renaissance traditions: on the one hand, he is, by the conventions of the Senecan revival, and likewise by the implications of the play's sources, the figure of the avenger (we may infer the stress of the *Ur-Hamlet,* for instance, from Lodge's famous reference to "ye ghost which cried so miserally at ye Theator, like an oister wife, *Hamlet, reuenge.*"); on the other, by his specification as courtier, soldier, and scholar, he is posited as a dramatic incarnation of the figure of the courtier. His *ethos* here looks toward the historical model of Bayard or Sidney, and toward the theoretical model supplied by Castiglione's *Il libro del Cortegiano.*

But the figure of Castiglione's courtier is not only brave, courteous, learned, and athletic; he is also oriented—as we realize from Bembo's accommodation of the Platonic "stayre of love" that rises from this world upward toward the realm of ideas—in his very conception oriented toward transcendence: is a figure toward paradise. "Thus the soule kindled in the most holy fire of true heavenly love," says Bembo, "fleeth to couple her selfe with the nature of Angels. . . . Let us therefore bend all our force and thoughtes of soule to this most holy light, that sheweth us the way which leadeth to heaven." Indeed, from its very inception in the literary past the character of Hamlet seems to have been oriented toward transcendence, for even the shadowy Amleth of Saxo Grammaticus was (as translated by Oliver Elton) "loth to be thought prone to lying about any matter." And for the Hamlet of Shakespeare the primordial question itself, "To be, or not to be," depends for its answer on transcendent directionality—depends on which course is "nobler in the mind."

But the figure of the courtier, by his orientation toward transcendence, is intrinsically irreconcilable with the figure of the avenger. Where the interest in, say, Hieronimo's revenge of his son is not *whether* he shall kill, but *how* he shall kill, Hamlet's revenge of his father—turn-about in more ways than one—is suspended from the momentous question, *ought?* If we disentangle ourselves from conventional responses, and survey the avenger figure from a human perspective, we will see that it is not remarkable at all that Hamlet is conceived as delaying the despatch of Claudius, but remarkable rather that murder, to a Flamineo or an Aaron, is so wholly the reaction of an automaton.

The play of *Hamlet,* by developing the conflict between the avenger and the courtier, both completes and rejects the Senecan tradition. But the immobilizing paradox of Hamlet's character is revealed still more deeply in existential terms if the play is taken also as an arena of decision. The question of "why?" with which an *Existenz* confronts a command for action, uncovers the necessary interconnection of decision and responsibility. When one decides for an action, he decides for its consequences as well; and indeed, the projected knowledge of its consequences is part of the decision itself.

Now in matters of daily decision we attempt to assess consequences by principles our teachers have imparted to us, or that we have learned by prior experience; but under greater stress we tend to act instinctively as our parents would have acted. We all prefer, however, to assume a congruence between, on the one hand, our "then and elsewhere" of pedagogic precept and learned experience, and, on the other, our "then and elsewhere" of inbred parental example. Where they do not coincide, we experience indecision; where they radically do not coincide, we experience agony. Usually one or the other will loom larger as a cause of action, and however reluctantly, we will choose to be guided by that stronger reason. But what do we do if the sources of our ability to estimate the meaning of a decision are in conflict, and then are each strengthened until each becomes incontrovertible? Are we not then in the plight of that tormented ass, tethered between two bales of hay, whose choice, by its difficulty, became a renowned topic for scholastic controversy?

It is into precisely such a dilemma of opposed responsibilities that Hamlet is plunged by the ghost's command. The motive core of the entire play resides in the fifth scene of the first act. "I am thy father's spirit," intones the ghost (I.v.9), summoning the reality of a "then and elsewhere" that, as Biblical commandments testify, and as Freud has demonstrated, and as almost all men have experienced, carries an enormous urgency in the "here and now." The full weight of all a father-son relationship can mean is remorselessly placed upon

Hamlet by the ghost: "List, Hamlet, O, list!/If thou didst ever thy dear father love—" (I.v.22–3), and Hamlet's reply, "O God!" confirms the impact any request must have if prefaced by such words. And then the ghost strikes home with his command: "Revenge his foul and most unnatural murder" (I.v.25). So that the "here and now" may receive the full responsibility of its burden, the ghost, on departing, leaves behind him a final exhortation that reverberates into the very corners of all "then and elsewhere," both of the past and of the future: "Adieu, adieu! Hamlet, remember me" (I.v.91).

So weighted, Hamlet can only acknowledge the inconceivable force of the command: "Remember thee!/Ay, thou poor ghost, while memory holds a seat/ In this distracted globe" (I.v.95–97). But next we hear the price of such memory, and if we understand the commitment of Hamlet's heaven-bent *Existenz,* we realize the bitter meaning of that price.

> Remember thee!
> Yea, from the table of my memory
> I'll wipe away all trivial fond records,
> All saws of books, all forms, all pressures past,
> That youth and observation copied there,
> And thy commandment all alone shall live
> Within the book and volume of my brain.
>
> (I.v.97–103)

To remember the ghost's command to revenge is to expunge all that Wittenberg means, all that Hamlet the scholar has learned and believed; these "trivial fond records"—and the litotes is cruel—are merely "All saws of books, all forms, all pressures past,/ That youth and observation copied there," are merely, that is, all that Hamlet has ever learned or has ever stood for or ever moved toward, are, in short, the entirety of his heaven-oriented education. The pride and dignity of his *Existenz*

—these are those "trivial fond records." To honor the "then and elsewhere" of the ghost's claim, which, made in the explicit context of a father's summoning up of past love and duty, is a claim upon nothing less than a son's defining sense of self—to honor such a claim, Hamlet must give up, not goods, no matter how rich, nor youth, no matter how bright, nor friends, nor approval, nor any of the other treasured affects of existence— rather, Hamlet must give up the movement of existence itself.

A chasm opens up at the ghost's command. We are astonished at the power and sureness of Shakespeare's intuition in making the confrontation of claims so colossal, and their implications so irreconcilable: the paradox of Hamlet's choice reverberates not only against the minutest scruples of his conscious reasoning but through the dimmest caverns of his subconscious motives.

In such a reverberation we become aware of another kind of hiddenness in the play. The tension of the "here and now" with the "then and elsewhere" involves vertical as well as horizontal perspectives. "Then" is hidden from "now" in the space and time of the play, but, additionally, action and attitude are hidden from their motive explanations in the objectified pattern of the play's character–encounters. "I have that within which passeth show," says Hamlet (I.ii.85); and it is for such reason that in the interpretation of his attitudes we turn to psychoanalysis for explicative help. The figure of the father, summoning up obligations from events past, commands not only the particular agonized response of Hamlet in this play, but points us toward correlatives, in our universal experience, that have been elucidated by Freud's description of the formation and development of human personality. And the virtue of the Freudian approach to *Hamlet* is not only that psychoanalysis is indispensable to an understanding of how the hidden relationships of the play cohere (though indispensable is a word so strong that we might not apply it to Freud's use for any other great work, excepting of course *Oedipus Rex* itself); its virtue also is that psychoanalysis complements, rather than wars against, other interpretations. Especially does Freudian explication augment the relevance of an existential interpretation, serving the realm of unconscious pattern as *Existenz* thought does the realm of conscious decision and responsibility.

Accordingly, to our understanding of the conscious alternatives of Hamlet's decision, we can add, through Freud's insight—notably as focused in Ernest Jones's *Hamlet and Oedipus*—a deepened sense of the ghost's monumental power. That psychic fact by which the existence of the father in the "then and elsewhere" is transmitted to the concern of the son in the "here and now" is illuminated by Freud as the phenomenon of identification. It is not merely that the ghost of Hamlet's father commands a son to an action (and the very ghosthood of the father is an ironic confirmation of the mysterious power of psychic residues in determining our lives), but by Freud's investigations we understand that a father becomes the son, that the son participates in the psychic reality of the father. The ghost's command is thereby Hamlet's own command, and involves his very existence.

We pause in wonder at Shakespeare's instinctive sureness in modifying his source to witness this truth. In Belleforest, Hamlet's father is a remote and loveless brigand named Horvendile:

> Now the greatest honor that men of noble birth could at that time win and obtaine, was in exercising the art of Piracie vpon the seas; assayling their neighbours . . . and how much the more they vsed to rob, pill, and spoyle other Prouinces, and Ilands farre adiacent, so much the more their honours and reputation increased . . . wherein Horuendile obtained the highest place in

his time, beeing the most renouned Pirate that in those dayes scoured the seas.

Even such a figure as Horvendile, aided by the force of the revenge convention, might exert disquieting pressure upon his offspring. But how mightily is such a pressure amplified when a father speaks to his son, named Hamlet, not in the guise of a barbarous absentee named Horvendile, but as an upright and just king named—in refocused identity—Hamlet!

But Shakespeare's intensification of the pressure on this side of the scale of decision is ironically matched by intensification on the other. Hamlet the father is not only a just and upright king, but a Christian king as well. From such a qualifying matrix there issue, with reverberations no less seismic than the exhortation to revenge, the imperatives of mankind's noblest and most influential conception of the moral concerns of existence. The ghost's power, stemming from the past, is incalculably huge. But incalculably huge also, and also stemming from the past, is Christianity's power of counter-exhortation. The ghost's cry, "remember me," is accepted by Hamlet as henceforth "my word" (I.v.110)—but the Christian faith conceives another "word," also given by a father. The ghost's plea for revenge is acccpted by Hamlet as henceforth "thy commandment" (I.v.102)— but the Christian faith recognizes one climactic "commandment" that stands in strictest opposition to such a commandment to revenge. "A new commandment I give unto you," says Christ, "That ye love one another" (John 13:34). "Dearly beloved," writes Paul, "avenge not yourselves . . . for it is written, Vengeance is mine; I will repay, saith the Lord" (Romans 12:19). "Ye have heard that it hath been said, An eye for an eye, and a tooth for a tooth," says Jesus, "But I say unto you, That ye resist not evil: but whosoever shall smite thee on thy right cheek, turn to him the other also" (Matthew 5:38–9). "Ye have heard that it hath been said, Thou shalt love thy neighbour, and hate thine enemy," continues Christ, "But I say unto you, Love your enemies" (Matthew 5:43–4). And, of course, there is the old and simple commandment, "Thou shalt not kill" (Exodus 20:13). Small wonder, then, that in the context of Christianity the ghost, all his fatherhood notwithstanding, seems nearer to Satan than to God: "The spirit that I have seen/ May be the devil," says Hamlet (II.ii.627–8)—and though on the surface this late conjecture seems merely a lame afterthought to eke out his reluctance to act, in ironic perspective the ghost's commandment is, in fact, plainly devilish.

Yet not only does the radical explicitness of the Christian gospel (and Nietzsche bears tormented witness to its power to dim the native hue of resolution even in minds most determined in unbelief) occupy the scale opposed to revenge, but to that scale is added also the weight of the view of man's dignity that, emanating from Greece rather than Israel, became the proud motivation of so much of the achievement of Renaissance humanism. "Wonders are many on earth," exults the great chorus in *Antigone,* "and the greatest of these is man. . . . He is master of ageless Earth. . . . He is lord of all things living. . . . There is nothing beyond his power." This exhilarated sense of man's unique worth, refracted through the centuries, surges upward again in the conceptions of the Renaissance, and it is in summation of a whole line of Renaissance thought that Hamlet marvels to Rosencrantz and Guildenstern:

> What a piece of work is a man! How noble in reason! How infinite in faculty, in form and moving! How express and admirable in action! How like an angel in apprehension! How like a god! The beauty of the world! The paragon of animals! (II.ii.315–9)

But the Renaissance emphasis on man's dignity, as Cassirer has shown in his masterful *Individuum und Kosmos in der Philosophie der Renaissance,* was pervasively characterized by a belief in the necessity of moral striving to maintain that dignity. The worth of man was not a given element in his nature, but a possibility in his function, and could be forfeited as well as fulfilled. From among many statements, one in Pico della Mirandola's *De hominis dignitate* may be taken as representative of this important qualification:

God the Father . . . built this cosmos we behold. . . . The place beyond the heavens He brightened with intelligences, the heavenly spheres with souls, and the earthy part of the lower world He filled with various kinds of being. But when the work was finished He wished that there was someone to appreciate it. . . . Finally He decreed that the creature who had nothing unique to himself should partake of all the different kinds of being. He therefore assigned man a place in the middle of the world, addressing him as follows: "Neither a fixed place nor a form that is yours alone nor any function peculiar to yourself have we given you, Adam, so that according to your desire and judgment you may have what place, what form, what function you yourself shall decide. . . . We have made you neither of heaven nor of earth, neither mortal nor immortal, so that with freedom of choice, as though you were your own maker, you must fashion your own shape. You can degenerate into the brutish form of the animals below you, and you can attain the divine and higher forms above you." O bounty of God! O wonderful happiness of man! To man it is given to have whatever he chooses, to be whatever he wills.

The power of man to choose his own being, which Pico here celebrates, is a capability not only of moving higher, but of falling lower, and it is because of this double possibility of his destiny that to existential choice man must add existential responsibility.

The moral conception, therefore, of the dignity of man's possibilities joins with the imperatives of Christian writ to stay Hamlet's hand. Not only does the dignity of man make the contemplation of the destruction of any man a difficult thought, but the transcendent base of that dignity makes all actions refer to the best possibility of self rather than the actual degeneration of others. When Polonius offers to lodge the players "according to their desert," Hamlet accordingly—and characteristically—says, "God's bodykins, man, better. Use every man after his desert, and who should scape whipping? Use them after your own honour and dignity" (II.ii.554–6).

Thus Hamlet delays. But not because decision as such is difficult—any psychopathic murderer's whimsical action tells us otherwise. It is easy enough to kill Claudius: a Lodovico and Gasparo are commonplace; faceless first, second, and third murderers clutter the *Dramatis Personae* of *Macbeth* as they do the annals of history. And it is likewise easy enough not to kill Claudius. What, excruciatingly, is not easy is the determination of the "ought," the moral dimension, of the action. Hamlet's action, aspiring to raise his existence toward transcendence, cannot be pure action. It must be action responsible to the future and to the past, that is, to the unity of his *Existenz*. It is fitting that we use the word "integrity" to mean not only wholeness, but specifically moral wholeness—for existentially speaking, morality is wholeness, and wholeness morality.

So it is that those tormented words that open the play—the "Who's there?" of Bernardo on the battlements—are not only the question of a struggling humanity to a dark cosmos, but pre-eminently the question of a "here and now" seeking its full integrity as *Existenz*. As such the question echoes and re-echoes as *basso ostinato* of the entire composition. When Polonius, to Laertes, riffles placidly through his catalogue of truisms—counseling properly, if not deeply, in matters of dress, deportment, management of funds, and other practicalities—he thinks to crown his advice by a final exhortation: "This above all: to thine own self be true,/ And it must follow, as the night the day,/ Thou canst not then be false to any man" (I.iii.78–80). As this advice, from another realm entirely than that of its preceding specifications, rolls off the old counselor's uncomprehending tongue, it catches up the initial "Who's there?" of Bernardo and poses mockingly the question that underlies all responsible choice. For choice, made from the existential standpoint of the "here and now," must always be faithful to an *Existenz* spanning the "then and elsewhere" of past and future—and, in fact, determines that *Existenz*. How to know what constitutes "thine own self,"—which Polonius, in his eagerness to round off his bromide, blandly takes as given—is the question that tears apart the life of Hamlet.

Indeed, the questioning of the humanistic tradition as signalized by the Delphic *gnothi seauton*—know thyself —unfolds a root irony of the play. "To thine own self be true," purrs Polonius in witless advice flung to the winds. "O wonderful happiness of man!" exults Pico, "To man it is given . . . to be whatever he wills." But what if a man wills such a self—loving and dutiful son, as well as humanist and Christian prince—that his situation suddenly splits into irreconcilable opposition? Of what avail then is the optimism of the Renaissance scholar or the truisms of Polonius? "O summum et admirandam hominis felicitatem! cui datum . . . id esse quod velit." But can Pico tell Hamlet what to choose? Can Polonius tell such a legatee of woe how to be true? "What should such fellows as I do," moans Hamlet, the courtier's, soldier's, scholar's pride humbled by a glimpse into the abyss—"what should such fellows as I do crawling between heaven and earth?" (III.i.129–30). "What should we do?" (I.iv.57).

Thus the final meanings of the play all rest upon the inseparability of decision from responsibility. The Freudian analyses of character relations show how the play coheres, but only the existential understanding of possibility, decision, and responsibility reveals what it means. The events of the play after Hamlet's meeting with the ghost are merely givens for the Freudian approach, though once they are given psychoanalysis can show their human plausibility. From an existential standpoint, however, we see these events not only as plausible, but as necessary to the meaning of Hamlet's dilemma.

For it is not only Hamlet who is confronted by the final question of Kant, "What ought I to do?" Every figure in the play is likewise the determinant of his own actions, and, with few exceptions, the decisions made by the other characters are decisions that attempt to avoid or truncate the responsibilities of *Existenz*.

It is the unprofitableness of such avoidance that is witnessed by the *exemplum* of Rosencrantz and Guildenstern. The two figures are outwardly casualties of the conflict between Hamlet and Claudius. " 'Tis dangerous," says Hamlet in cool dismissal of their destruction, "when the baser nature comes/ Between the pass and fell incensed points/ Of mighty opposites" (V.ii.60–2). Yet they are not so much destroyed by Hamlet's ruthlessness as by their own dereliction of responsibility; they are "the enginer/ Hoist with his own petar" (III.iv.206–7), and are accordingly—or so at least Hamlet says—"not near my conscience" (V.ii.58).

The responsibility they forfeit is their friendship with Hamlet, but at the same time their own *Existenz*. For in attempting to assure their future (by becoming a sponge "that soaks up the King's countenance, his rewards, his authorities" [IV.ii.16–17]), they disown their past. The initial price that "Rosencrantz and gentle Guildenstern," and "Guildenstern and gentle Rosencrantz" pay for their abandonment of friendship's dignity is loss of identity—such, we realize, is the significance and mockery of their doubling as one character.

It is important to understand that their betrayal of their past with Hamlet is a violation of a deep commitment. As Gertrude says, "Good gentlemen, he hath much talk'd of you;/ And sure I am two men there are not living/ To whom he more adheres" (II.ii.19–21). And Hamlet's greeting to the pair vindicates the queen's words: "My excellent good friends! How dost thou, Guildenstern? Oh, Rosencrantz! Good lads, how do ye both?" (II.ii.228–30). So great, indeed, is his gladness that we glimpse for a moment the humane and gentle Hamlet of "then and elsewhere." For Hamlet, however, the dignity of friendship is inseparable from responsibility to such friendship—implies "obligation" to the past and future of "ever-preserved love":

> *Ham.* I know the good king and queen have sent for you.
> *Ros.* To what end, my lord?
> *Ham.* That you must teach me. But let me conjure you by the rights of our fellowship, by the consonancy of our youth, by the obligation of our ever-preserved love . . . be even and direct with me. . . .   (II.ii.290–8)

The extent, and seriousness, of the two false friends' existential dereliction is focused by the figure of the true friend: Horatio. Like LaFeu in *All's Well,* however, Horatio, though serving as measure of what man ought to be, is curiously ineffectual, strangely closed off from the problems of the play. He, like Hamlet, is a representative of Wittenberg, but Hamlet alone partakes of the torment of Elsinore. Standing at Hamlet's shoulder, as it were, Horatio offers sympathy, but little help. Nonetheless, in a world of disloyalty, broken faith, deceit, and

murder, he is a fleeting and inconclusive figure of human
integrity. Though ironically inactive, he serves to reveal Hamlet's ideal of "honour and dignity" as a social,
not merely an individual, possibility. Horatio extends
the ideal of human dignity, and thereby validates
friendship and the conception of the responsibilities attendant upon the choosing of human relationships. Thus
Hamlet, in a fervent passage, emphasizes that Horatio
has been

> As one, in suffering all, that suffers nothing,
> A man that Fortune's buffets and rewards
> Hath ta'en with equal thanks; and blest are those
> Whose blood and judgement are so well commingled,
> That they are not a pipe for Fortune's finger
> To sound what stop she pleases. Give me that man
> That is not passion's slave, and I will wear him
> In my heart's core, ay, in my heart of heart,
> As I do thee.   (III.ii.71–9)

Such praise simultaneously emphasizes the falseness of Rosencrantz and Guildenstern. The image with
which Hamlet urges Horatio's integrity—"not a pipe for
Fortune's finger/ To sound what stop she pleases"—is,
we realize, the same image with which he most fully expresses his contempt for men who violate the responsibilities of friendship. "Will you play upon this pipe?"
asks Hamlet, proffering a recorder. "My lord, I cannot.
. . . I know no touch of it," says Guildenstern uneasily.
" 'Tis easy as lying," counters Hamlet in acid scorn,
"Look you, these are the stops." "I have not the skill,"
protests Guildenstern. "Why, look you now," says Hamlet savagely, "how unworthy a thing you make of me!
You would play upon me, you would seem to know my
stops . . . do you think that I am easier to be play'd on
than a pipe? Call me what instrument you will, though
you can fret me, you cannot play upon me" (III.-
ii.365–88).

Thus, seeking a Machiavellian future, Rosencrantz and Guildenstern betray their friendship's past. But their shifts before the winds of Fortune do not save them from destruction. The nobility of Hamlet resides in the paradox that rather than dishonor either one of two legitimate claims upon his existence, he delays, and in rending himself displays the extent of his commitment in life. In order, however, to accept his course as not only noble but also not foolish, we must see that more flexible or facile behavior likewise does not succeed in negotiating the abyss that surrounds existence. The failure, therefore, of Rosencrantz and Guildenstern, the men guided by self-interest and the main chance, authenticates Hamlet's moral inaction.

In the involvements of the play, however, that inaction results in a spreading torment that affects all the characters except the remote Horatio. Now the individual uglinesses attendant upon Hamlet's encounters are, in one aspect of their meaning, the measure of his concern. As psychic manifestations they cohere by Freudian explication; but Hamlet's rage and abuse toward Ophelia, his hatred and sarcasm toward Polonius, his ferocious censure of his mother, his cold unconcern at the deaths of Polonius and his two former friends—all these marks of agonized inner conflict bespeak the hugeness of the aspirations that have been blocked. The destruction caused by Hamlet attests the extent of his flailing agony of spirit—as it does the insolubility of his dilemma. "A man's free choice," says Augustine in *De spiritu et littera*,

> avails only to lead him to sin, if the way of truth be hidden from him. And when it is plain to him what he should do and to what he should aspire, even then, unless he feel delight and love therein, he does not perform his duty, nor undertake, nor attain the good life.

Hamlet cannot see his way, and his choices do not attain for him the good life. But his rage is an index of his seriousness; his remorselessness, an index of his idealism.

Yet, in another aspect of their meaning the troubled events of the play descry not only Hamlet's agony but the derelictions of its other characters. For in this play we learn again and again that if Hamlet's noble indecision solves none of his problems, the others' contrastingly ignoble decisiveness, or evasion of decision's responsibility, solves none for them either.

Thus, the inexorable bond of decision and responsibility is asserted, ironically and terribly, by the destruction of Polonius's entire family.

The introduction of Laertes, Ophelia, and Polonius in the third scene of the first act, following as it does upon the dismal scene that opens the play, and upon our initial view of how weary, stale, flat and unprofitable Hamlet's "here and now" has become, is like a happy chirruping of birds in the morning. This family, so affectionate, blending so desirably eager youth and indulgent age, so cheerful, so normal, seems to dispel the gloom and the forebodings of the first scene, and to rebuke the melancholy of the second. But as the play unfolds, we see all its members attempting to separate decision from responsibility.

Hence Laertes, who has heretofore existed in the play as a seemingly worthy rival of Hamlet for the laurels of youth and ability, and who, from a Freudian perspective, is a sibling figure against whom Hamlet contends for identity, is confronted in the fourth act with a sister dead and a father murdered. The same code of revenge that the ghost has tendered to Hamlet is proffered to Laertes. "What would you undertake," asks Claudius, "To show yourself your father's son in deed/ More than in words?" (IV.vii.125–7). Laertes, grasping the cup eagerly, answers with ready decisiveness: "To cut his throat i' th' church" (IV.vii.127). The unconscious irony of Claudius's Machiavellian benediction to this decision ("No place, indeed, should murder sanctuarize;/ Revenge should have no bounds" [IV.vii.128–9]) accentuates the chaos that comes from response without responsibility; for had Hamlet then, in his response to the ghost, heeded Claudius's ethic of revenge as here declared, Claudius, the counselor to revenge, would long since have been cast into nonexistence.

So Laertes chooses, yet his choice brings him neither worldly success nor satisfaction, and it strips him of his dignity. In short minutes, the valiant and troubled son who strode before Claudius and said "Give me my father!" (IV.v.116) has made a decision divorced from responsibility and hence from dignity: "To this point I stand,/ That both the worlds I give to negligence,/ Let come what comes; only I'll be reveng'd/ Most thoroughly for my father" (IV.v.133–6). Its concern thus dissipated in negligence, the existence of Laertes collapses from courtier to grotesque automaton of revenge: "with a little shuffling," suggests Claudius, "you may choose/ A sword unbated, and in a pass of practice/ Requite him for your father" (IV.vii.138–40). But the king's practiced treachery is topped by the Ithamore-like eagerness of the self-abandoned Laertes: "I will do't;/ And, for that purpose, I'll anoint my sword./ I bought an unction of a mountebank" (IV.vii.140–2).

If Laertes deserts the courtier's responsibility in a situation rivalling that of Hamlet, Polonius is derelict in another way. In the Freudian schematization of the play Polonius is the decomposed father figure: a ludicrous live father in place of the awesome dead one, and therefore a focus for the hatred and resentment that are repressed in the relationship with the real father. The real father, as the play makes clear, is a "then and elsewhere" preserved almost worshipfully in Hamlet's mind. Thus, in the first act, before knowledge of the murder, Hamlet invokes his father as "So excellent a king; that

was, to this/ Hyperion to a satyr" (I.ii.139–40) and in
the third act as "A combination and a form indeed,/
Where every God did seem to set his seal/ To give the
world assurance of a man" (III.iv.60–2). Though Hamlet's respect for the "gracious figure" (III.iv.104) of his
father provides, on the one hand, the basis of the ghost's
extreme power, by the same token it also implies the
suppression of large resentments, which are discharged
on Polonius. "These tedious old fools!," says Hamlet
(II.ii.223), and we note the plural as the singular Polonius departs. "Is it the King?" (III.iv.26) asks Hamlet
ambivalently after stabbing the eavesdropper behind the
arras. And his remark to Polonius's corpse continues
ambiguous—ferociously so: "Thou wretched, rash, in-
truding fool, farewell!/ I took thee for thy better"
(III.iv.31–2). The "better," we understand, especially in
view of Hamlet's reluctance to proceed against Claudius
himself, as deeply refers to the Oedipally hated ghost
(who, when alive, had been "so loving to my mother"
[I.ii.140]) as to the present king.

And yet, though the Freudian view of Polonius is rich
in ironic nuance, it does not account for one large meaning of his role in the play. Polonius is not simply a
meddling old man, nor even a father substitute, but specifically a counselor—a man, that is, who helps in the
making of decisions. The irony of his function is not that
he is stupid—for he is old rather than stupid—and not
that his advice is bad advice. His conjecture, for instance,
that Hamlet is mad with love—"This is the very ecstasy
of love" (II.i.102)—is a reasonable one; his advice to
Laertes is, if platitudinous, soundly so; his reasons for
urging Ophelia to break off with Hamlet are ones that
any parent might approve—"I fear'd he did but trifle"
(II.i.112). The irony of Polonius's function is rather
that in offering counsel to others he tries to shape decisions without accepting responsibilities. And he has
no help for final problems. We see the triviality and ir-

relevance of his concern when, in ironic doubling of Claudius's dispatch of the embassy to Norway, Polonius, acting merely for the sake of action, instructs Reynaldo to go to Paris and spy on Laertes—but instructs him with no true purpose. "But, my good lord—" protests Reynaldo. Polonius anticipates the question: "Wherefore should you do this?" "Ay, my lord, I would know that." But Polonius, when held to account for the consequences of decision, drifts off: "And then, sir, does he this—he does—/ What was I about to say? By the mass, I was about to say something" (II.i.35–52).

Polonius's willingness to counsel, and to act, without true assumption of responsibility, interlocks with the dereliction of Ophelia. Where Laertes decides with alacrity, Ophelia seems not to decide at all. But in fact she does decide—she decides to let her father decide for her. "I would not," says Polonius to his daughter, ". . . Have you . . . give words or talk with the Lord Hamlet" (I.-iii.132–4). And Ophelia's abdication of responsibility, masked as filial duty, is signalized by five demurely unquestioning words: "I shall obey, my lord." (I.iii.136). When her father later asks if she has given Hamlet "any hard words of late?" she replies, still demure and still rejecting responsibility, "No, my good lord, but, as you did command,/ I did repel his letters and deni'd/ His access to me" (II.i.108–10).

And just as Laertes is presented with an exhortation to vengeance that parallels the one presented to Hamlet, so is Ophelia presented with an exhortation to memory that parallels the ghost's plea to "remember me" (I.v.91). "Farewell, Ophelia, and remember well," says Laertes, "What I have said to you" (I.iii.84–5)—and his urging, that Ophelia be wary of Hamlet, prefigures Polonius's successful interference. Neither the response of Laertes nor the response of Ophelia fails to accord with its exhortation—but neither Laertes nor Ophelia is thereby more successful than Hamlet.

Ophelia is the most hidden of all the drama's characters—as though, by her refusal to accept the responsibility of decision, she forsakes participation as well. In this regard, she stands outside the play and looks in. From inside the play we see her, as it were, standing outside at a window. Then her lovely form withdraws, reappearing later at another window—but now mysteriously agonized. Then again she passes from view, rounds the corner of the house, and at yet another window acts out the pathetic destruction of her reason and life. Her sweetness, her blamelessness of ill intent, do not avail her in the face of the terrible law of decision and responsibility.

From a Freudian standpoint, we understand Hamlet's abuse of Ophelia as in part his resentment toward his mother; and we understand his lack of ardor toward Ophelia as corollary to his psychic bondage to his mother. But from an existential standpoint we understand that Ophelia does not observe the fundamental responsibilities that hold together an existence. To our dismayed question as to why this girl, young, gentle, complaisant, should be destroyed—"for what did she ever do?"—an ironic answer presents itself: "nothing."

If Ophelia attempts to hide from existence behind femininity and youth, Gertrude, her counterpoise, though equally passive in her overt role in the play, is much more deliberate in her own rejection of responsibility. Where Ophelia evades responsibility from a kind of ignorance of the laws of *Existenz,* Gertrude, much harder behind her softness, understands matters very well, but simply, and stunningly, does not care. Thus where Polonius, the professional sage, identifies Hamlet's madness as lovesickness, and where the coldly watchful Claudius is unable to come to any conclusion about its cause, Gertrude, casual and insouciant, identifies the exact and precise nature of the situation. "He tells me, my sweet queen," says Claudius as Polonius departs, "that he hath found/ The head and source of all your son's distemper" (II.ii.54–5)—to which Gertrude, almost offhandedly, replies (and the play stands still) "I doubt it is no other but the main,/ His father's death and our o'erhasty marriage" (II.ii.56–7). She understands; but she does not care.

This terrible, this existence-destroying, nonchalance is the hallmark of Gertrude's character—not ill will, bad temper, evil designs, ambition, vengefulness, wicked passion, or other of the usual motivations of such formidable dramatic creations as Videna, Tamora, Lady Macbeth, or Beatrice-Joanna. By her "o'erhasty" marriage Gertrude has wrought no physical harm; she is guiltless of collusion in her first husband's death; she has pleasant words for all. But by her shortening of the mourning time for her dead husband she disowns the meaning of the past. She shows that she did not, and does not, care. She disclaims the dignity of Hamlet's father; she disclaims the integrity of her own *Existenz*. It is scarcely by accident that in almost all societies custom prescribes deep and reverential periods of mourning after the death of a person dear to others; the instinct for the preservation of the past's meaning is inseparable from that care for existence out of which all conceptions of human dignity arise. But in this play the act of social reverence for the meaning of the past—a funeral—is ironically merged with a disjointed claim upon the future: a marriage. Such a collapse of human dimension is witnessed in a passage of searing bitterness:

Hor. My lord, I came to see your father's funeral.
Ham. I pray thee, do not mock me, fellow-student
I think it was to see my mother's wedding.
Hor. Indeed, my lord, it followed hard upon.
Ham. Thrift, thrift, Horatio! The funeral bak'd meats
Did coldly furnish forth the marriage tables.

(I.ii.176–81)

For Hamlet, a human life is not merely a "now," but a "then" of the past, and a "then" of the future, and the concern for the full range of this existence is not merely the burden of man, but his dignity and distinction from the beasts. A "beast, that wants discourse of reason,/ Would have mourn'd longer" (I.ii.150–1) than did his mother; and her action, by its contempt for human meaning, is, despite its lack of malignant intention, in a certain and philosophical sense worse than that of Claudius. "What is a man," asks her heaven-aspiring son,

> If his chief good and market of his time
> Be but to sleep and feed? A beast, no more.
> Sure, He that made us with such large discourse,
> Looking before and after, gave us not
> That capability and god-like reason
> To fust in us unus'd.

(IV.iv.33–9)

Gertrude, by her lack of care for the "before and after," threatens all meanings. Indeed, the very being of existence, as Heidegger maintains, is care ("Das Sein des Daseins ist die Sorge"). In homage to the "before and after" Hamlet is willing to rend his life—the ghost's burning "Do not forget!" (III.iv.110) derives its special power from its appeal to the "large discourse" of Hamlet's transcendence-oriented mind, to his "reason" in its "god-like" concern. Thus, Gertrude's sweetly vacuous question to her son, "What have I done . . .?" outbrazens, almost, the act of Claudius. "What have I done, that thou dar'st wag thy tongue/ In noise so rude against me?" (III.iv.39–40). Hamlet's reply is marked by the deepest intensity of outrage:

> Such an act
> That blurs the grace and blush of modesty
> . . . O, such a deed
> As from the body of contraction plucks

> The very soul, and sweet religion makes
> A rhapsody of words.

> (III.iv.40–8)

It is not enough to see in such a statement, with its special emphasis on the forfeiture of meaning, solely the indication of an Oedipal jealousy. For the fact glossed over by Freudian interpretation is that Gertrude's remarriage, by any standard of human meaning, does in truth constitute an outrage. It is not a marriage in due course, after a reverential period of mourning, but an "o'erhasty" marriage—as she herself demurely admits; it "followed hard upon" the death of her husband—as Horatio tactfully says; the mourning period was a "little month" (I.ii.147)—as Hamlet states. No, Gertrude acts without scruple. She abandons the claims of the past. She attempts to live in a perpetual present, and thereby to solve all problems. But when the future of the tragedy arrives, Gertrude's solution is revealed as no more successful than those of her fellows. As Hamlet is wracked to a bitter darkness, as the family of Polonius is destroyed, Gertrude too, clutching at "now," sinks to death.

If Gertrude's uncaringness intensifies Hamlet's agony, her pliant presence likewise complicates the role of Claudius. In the Freudian conception of that role, Claudius, by acting out the Oedipal fantasy of killing the father and marrying the mother, becomes the psychodramatic representative of Hamlet himself. Hamlet's delay is therefore the hesitancy of the man asked to kill, not merely another, but himself as well. Nonetheless, though the Freudian interpretation adds to our understanding of Hamlet's delay—illuminates the question "Why does Hamlet take so long to kill Claudius?"—it sheds no light on a counter question that is almost no less pressing: "Why does Claudius take so long to kill Hamlet?"

Why indeed does Claudius take so long to kill Hamlet? The fact that the king cannot suspect—at least until after the play-within-the-play—that Hamlet has knowledge of his father's murder is no adequate reason to delay Hamlet's own assassination; for every aspirant to power knows—to borrow the words of Mendoza, the Machiavel in *The Malcontent*—that "Prevention is the heart of policy." "Shall we murder him?" "Instantly?" "Instantly! Before he casts a plot"—such prompt forehandedness is the primer lesson of Machiavellianism. Yet Claudius does not remove Hamlet at once, does not act against him until too late.

Now when asked, by Laertes, "why you proceed not" against Hamlet, Claudius gives two explanations for his atypical behavior:

> O, for two special reasons,
> Which may to you, perhaps, seem much unsinew'd,
> And yet to me they are strong. The Queen his mother
> Lives almost by his looks; and for myself—
> My virtue or my plague, be it either which—
> She's so conjunctive to my life and soul,
> That, as the star moves not but in his sphere,
> I could not but by her. The other motive
> Why to a public count I might not go
> Is the great love the general gender bear him
>
> (IV.vii.9–18)

And yet the answer is in part misleading, for only the first of the reasons can be considered valid. Though the second reason might discourage Claudius from public action, it would by no means prevent the secret action of the Machiavel. Indeed, Claudius has already sent Hamlet to England with "letters conjuring to that effect,/ The present death of Hamlet" (IV.iii.66–7). The first reason alone, therefore, seems to account for the fact that Claudius, in despatching Hamlet's father, did not at the same time make himself forever secure by removing the son.

Claudius, in brief, loves Gertrude. This truth, so easily granted from one standpoint, uncovers the deepest ironic ramifications of his Machiavellian *ethos*. For just as Hamlet's heavenly progress founders on the call to revenge, so does Claudius's earthly policy founder on the call to love. Revenge, which has no place in Christian commitment, obtrudes nonetheless in Hamlet's concern; love, which has no place in Machiavellian commitment, obtrudes nonetheless in the concern of Claudius.

Claudius is the classic Machiavel—except for his love. He "did the murder," as he says, for "My crown, mine own ambition, and my queen" (III.iii.54–5). The first two reasons are normal for the Machiavel; yet the third is an anomaly. "My utmost project," says Mendoza, "is to murder the duke, that I might have his state." Such, and no more, is the aspiration of the Machiavellian *ethos*. Indeed, the Machiavel is specifically enjoined from spiritual preoccupation, and above all, from love. "I will teach thee," says Barabas to Ithamore in Machiavellian catechism: "First, be thou void of these affections:/ Compassion, love, vain hope, and heartless fear;/ Be mov'd at nothing, see thou pity none." And Richard of Gloucester, in *III Henry VI,* gloats that he has "neither pity, love, nor fear" (V.vi.68). Thus, like Richard, who can "smile, and murder whiles I smile" *(III Henry VI,* III.ii.182), Claudius can "smile, and smile, and be a villain" (I.v.108). Like Richard, who can "set the murderous Machiavel to school" *(III Henry VI,* III.ii.193), Claudius is without scruple in his quest for power. But unlike Richard, Claudius cannot say that "since this earth affords no joy to me/ But to command . . . I'll make my heaven to dream upon the crown" *(III Henry VI,* III.ii.165–8). Though Claudius forfeits a Christian heaven for his dream of a crown, his relationship with Gertrude introduces a new and unaccountable dimension into his experience. "Love," says Richard, "forswore me in my mother's womb" *(III Henry VI,* III.ii.153). But Gertrude, for Claudius, is "conjunctive to my life and soul" (IV.vii.14).

Therefore, just as Hamlet's assumption of filial responsibility—an attitude which in ordinary situations would be a virtue—ironically leads to his destruction, so Claudius's capacity to love—again in ordinary situations a virtue—lures his own ship onto the rocks. And it must be emphasized that Claudius's love can in no way be seen as other than a destructive anomaly in his total commitment, for Claudius's Machiavellianism, against which his love works, is intrinsic to his character—is the sole guarantee of that grandeur, that defining largeness of existence, which allows him to be Hamlet's "mighty opposite." For, like Hamlet, Claudius does not try to escape existence. Where Gertrude attempts to evade the past and its responsibilities, and where Ophelia does the same in terms of the future, Claudius, like Hamlet, accepts past, future, and responsibility. Recognizing that "my offence is rank," that "It hath the primal eldest curse upon't,/ A brother's murder," he does not refuse to accept the meaning of the deed:

> But, O, what form of prayer
> Can serve my turn? "Forgive me my foul murder?"
> That cannot be; since I am still possess'd
> Of those effects for which I did the murder,
> My crown, mine own ambition, and my queen.
>
> (III.iii.51–5)

Such impressive honesty is an appurtenance of Claudius's Machiavellian commitment. Indeed, it is a primary feature of Machiavellianism that its aspirations are no less demanding, its coherence no less total, than the aspirations and coherence of Christianity—Machiavellianism is in fact, as Gentillet's *Contre-Machiavel* and

Donne's *Ignatius His Conclave* emphasize, precisely the mortal competitor of Christianity. "I count religion but a childish toy," says the prolocutor, Machiavelli, of *The Jew of Malta*—for "Might first made kings." The power of earthly rule thus supplants heaven as transcendent goal, and all subordinate values are recast to service this shift in the conception of life's purpose. York, in *II Henry VI,* is prepared "when I spy advantage" to "claim the crown,/ For that's the golden mark I seek to hit." "And, father, do but think," echoes his son in *III Henry VI,* "How sweet a thing it is to wear a crown/ Within whose circuit is Elysium/ And all that poets feign of bliss and joy." The emphasis on "Elysium" reveals an aspiration on the part of the Machiavel that is no less unflinching than that of the Christian—an aspiration in whose service the whole of *Existenz* is mobilized. "Nature," as Marlowe states, "Doth teach us all to have aspiring minds," and as Machiavels we "wear ourselves and never rest/ Until we reach the ripest fruit of all,/ That perfect bliss and sole felicity,/ The sweet fruition of an earthly crown."

As Hamlet, therefore, is a dramatic embodiment, in the tradition of the Courtier, of aspiration toward the spiritual transcendence of heaven, Claudius, in the competing tradition of the Machiavel, witnesses an aspiration toward earthly power. By rejecting the spirit, and the morality of "honour and dignity," the Machiavel thinks to come to terms with existence. And yet, though the ideals of the Courtier do not keep Hamlet from shipwreck, neither, ironically, do the ruthless pragmatisms of Claudius's Machiavellian commitment steer his own *Existenz* through to safety. Claudius, like Hamlet, finds all his abilities inadequate in a paradoxical boundary situation. With the uncle, as with the nephew, the ironies of life divide the understanding and dissipate the illusion of a right way. If for Hamlet, cast into a situation of disharmony, there is truly no exit, the radically different postulates of the Machiavel likewise provide no keys to the final doors of existence.

Thus, as Hamlet delays, suspended between his two choices, the theme of decision and responsibility is taken up for other characters and situations of the play. We are led to realize that for the other figures no amelioration of attitude, no variation of stance, resolves problems with any truer success than that achieved by Hamlet himself. Indeed, the yawning grave of Ophelia, with which the fifth act of *Hamlet* opens, is emblematic of the only doors opened by the differing efforts of the play's humanity.

In the course of the fifth act, however, the indecision of Hamlet is ironically resolved; and the tragedy swirls toward a bleak and dreadful conclusion.

The act is divided into two distinct sections—the grave-digger scene, on the one hand, and the sequence of events that lead up to the deaths of Hamlet and Claudius on the other. These parts raise themselves to less elevation of spirit and hope than does the conclusion of any other of Shakespeare's great tragedies; indeed, in a sense *Hamlet* dips down—to the humor of the grave-digger scene, to the melodrama of the final duel. Yet we cannot doubt the efficacy of the act's service to the meaning of the play.

The second part of the act, which deals with the duel and its preparations, stands in the starkest contrast to the motifs of hiddenness in the play's earlier movement. Now all is surface: Hamlet and Laertes leaping into Ophelia's grave, Hamlet's extended repartee with Osric, the details of the swordplay, with the stage business of poisoned rapier and poisoned wine. In terms of dramatic effect, the rapidity and flamboyance of this concluding section serve as relief to the long-continued hiddenness and contemplation typical of the play's earlier development. And in terms of meaning, the final action indicates, by its lack of overtone, the ironic truth that the shattering reverberations of Hamlet's dilemma have at last been muffled. Thus, the second part of the act abandons the tortured questionings of earlier situations; it becomes a kind of vortex in which Hamlet, Claudius, Laertes, and Gertrude—really without regard to what each of them does or does not do, decides or does not decide—descend to the termination of their existences. Hamlet kills Claudius without ever clearly making the full choice to do so—Claudius, as had Polonius, dies in the heat of passionate events. We can scarcely recall the order of occurrences by which the four characters meet death, or the means by which they die, so devoid of significance do their ends seem to be. And this sense of a sudden, and universal, pitching downward toward death follows psychologically from the revelations of the grave-digger scene.

This startling scene never exhausts its wonders. We come to its colossal humor direct from the heartbreaking pathos of Ophelia's death. If we thought our downcast eyes could spy, from the opening elevation of the battlements of Elsinore, the futurity of an open grave, how little did we expect this mad change in perspective. For now our standpoint, at the opening of this scene, is in the grave itself, looking out. And the opaqueness we now view is not the unanswerability of death, but the absurdity of life. The death's-head grin of the skulls jokingly presents us, after we thought we had identified the poles of possible meaning in Hamlet's choices, with a final—and freezing—possibility. To kill Claudius is a horrible thing from the perspective of the humanist; not to kill Claudius is a horrible thing from the perspective of the loyal son. For four acts the unspeakable pressures of the opposed commands have agonized the existences of Hamlet and his peers. But, at the beginning of the fifth act, as death the jester winks broadly, a final possibility uncovers itself—that of no meaning at all. To the question, "Ought I to kill Claudius?" the skulls at Hamlet's feet grin the suggestion of an unthinkable possibility: "It makes no difference."

For all here is humorously one. The crown of human reason, stripped to bare bone, is tossed jovially about, both by the sexton's spade and by such terms of playful contempt as "mazzard" and "sconce." "Where be his quiddits now," muses Hamlet of a skull that may have been a lawyer,

> his quillets, his cases, his tenures, and his tricks? Why does he suffer this rude knave now to knock him about the sconce with a dirty shovel, and will not tell him of his action of battery? Hum! This fellow might be in's time a great buyer of land, with his statutes, his recognizances, his fines, his double vouchers, his recoveries. Is this the fine of his fines, and the recovery of his recoveries, to have his fine pate full of fine dirt?
>
> (V.i.107–16)

Where "fine" as pretentiously meaningful legal event becomes "fine" in the sense of final end, where "recovery" as portentous legality becomes the cover of dirt, all value emphases and hierarchies of life dissolve. In existential jest Alexander the Great is imagined as dust stopping a bunghole, while the tanner, who "will last you nine year" (V.i.183–4) as a corpse before rotting, becomes, in the absurd counter-hierarchy of death, the head of society, and the shoveling clown its only lawgiver.

With this awesome scene, the alternatives that deadlocked into Hamlet's delay are loosened. The question, "ought I to kill Claudius?" is not resolved; it is, rather, diminished by the final possibility of unimportance. Instead of uncovering an elemental bifurcation of existence, the question of Hamlet, laughingly covered with the dirt of the grave-digger's shovel, possibly serves, in a third meaning that humbles meaning, as a witness to indifference. "I have seen all the works that are done under the sun," writes the Biblical Preacher, "and, behold all is vanity and vexation of spirit. . . . All go unto one place; all are of the dust, and all turn to dust again. . . . For who knoweth what is good for man in this life, all the days of his vain life which he spendeth as a shadow?" The musings and indecision of Hamlet have been a frantically personal obbligato in the Senecan movement of revenge. Now at last their sound is stilled, the skulls grin, and the play moves toward its universal night.

The Anxiety of Othello

Dr. Johnson found the murder of Desdemona too dreadful to be endured. Such a reaction to the cumulative effect of *Othello* points us toward a recognition of an important truth about its tragic tone: that the agonizing of the spirit that occurs in this play is, alone among the greatest Shakespearean tragedies, not accompanied by a corresponding elevation. Where *Antony and Cleopatra* and *King Lear* lift themselves linguistically into a gladness that serves as a paradoxical nullification of the increasing woes encountered in their action, and where *Hamlet,* though its language is less soaringly affirmative, nonetheless evokes in full measure our awareness of human nobility, *Othello* excruciatingly—indeed, up to the point of the Moor's great summarizing speech at the very end of the play—"Soft you; a word or two before you go"—twists and depresses the spectacle of human life. "What instruction can we make out of this Catastrophe?" asks Rymer of Desdemona's murder, "Is not

this to envenome and sour our spirits, to make us repine
and grumble at Providence and the government of the
World? If this be our end, what boots it to be Vertuous?"

This idiosyncratic lack of elevation is mirrored in a
much-noted feature of the play's diction, one that is
bound up with a curious and unpleasant psychological
closeness in its character interactions. The "vapour of a
dungeon" hangs over the semantic reference of *Othello*.
From the grotesque overtones of Iago's

> . . . I lay with Cassio lately;
> And, being troubled with a raging tooth,
> I could not sleep. . . .
> In sleep I heard him say, "Sweet Desdemona"
> . . . then lay his leg
> Over my thigh, and sigh, and kiss
>
> (III.iii.413–25)

to Othello's horrible interview with Desdemona,

> *Des.* My lord, what is your will?
> *Oth.*   Pray, chuck, come hither.
> *Des.* What is your pleasure? . . .
>   What horrible fancy's this?
> *Oth.* [To Emilia] Some of your function, mistress;
>   Leave procreants alone and shut the door;
>   Cough, or cry "hem," if anybody come
>
> (IV.ii.24–9)

—from one such situation to another, a fetid suggestive-
ness issues from the language of the play. It not only
surrounds the speech of the wicked Iago, but it permeates much of the language of the tragic protagonist himself: "This hand is moist, my lady. . . . Hot, hot,
and moist" (III.iv.36–9); "Damn her, lewd minx!"
(III.iii.475); "Goats and monkeys!" (IV.i.274); or, as we
near a perigee of all Shakespearean tragic utterance:

> Lie with her! lie on her! We say lie on her, when they
> belie her. Lie with her! Zounds, that's fulsome!—

Handkerchief—confessions—handkerchief. . . .Pish!
Noses, ears, and lips.—Is't possible?—Confess—
handkerchief!—O devil! (IV.i.35–44)

If we reflect on the pervasiveness of this degradation
of utterance, we find its norm to be established in the
first scene of the play, where, standing in the street, Iago,
in words that for the sheer shock of obscenity outdo most
efforts of deliberate pornography, taunts Brabantio at his
window: "an old black ram/ Is tupping your white ewe"
(I.i.88–9); "you'll have your daughter cover'd with a
Barbary horse; you'll have your nephews neigh to you;
you'll have coursers for cousins, and gennets for ger-
mans" (I.i.111–14); "I am one, sir, that comes to tell you
your daughter and the Moor are now making the beast
with two backs" (I.i.116–18). Such bestial reference
differs from the animal comparisons of *King Lear* in one
marked respect: the language of Iago is characterized
by a tone of mockery. And this fact of tone, added to
the situation itself, seems to suggest, in grotesque refrac-
tion, that coarse and jeeringly sexual wedding celebra-
tion known as *charivari*—a folk-ritual that we associate
not with high meaning from the standpoint of the individual, but with a shared recognition, from the huddled
herd of mankind, of animal realities beneath the formal
pretences of human relationships. In its denial of the
idealism of love, its affirmation—and salutation—of
the common lusts of mankind, this echo of the social
tone of *charivari* makes us aware of a strange truth
about the structure of *Othello:* that its tragic agony stems
from a plot that is simply an intensification of perhaps
the most recurrent of all comic themes. For Othello and
Desdemona are January and May, are the pantaloon and
the virgin, are the universally mocked spectacle of the
mismated marriage—the man too old, lustily bound to
the nubile woman he cannot service. Indeed, Nicoll, in
The World of Harlequin, emphasizes the early type of

the pantaloon figure in a way that strikingly pertains to Othello. Thus, *Pantalone* is a Venetian, and though he is "a 'vecchio,' an old man," he "is far from decrepitude." On the contrary, he is possessed of a "keen intelligence," and—as early portraits testify—of a "remarkable physique" with "brawny thighs and limbs." The *pantalone* figure is not "the knock-kneed rheumatic scarecrow erroneously described for us" by later tradition, but a "vigorous and downright middle-aged" man—a man, like Othello, "with a fine career behind him, who has become involved in an emotional world with which he cannot always cope."

But wherever it occurs, whether in the skits of *commedia dell' arte,* or in that muddy pastoral called *fabliau,* in the tales of Boccaccio or the moral comedies of Ben Jonson, the pantaloon-style mismatch is ridiculed by laughing at the over-age husband, and society returns to its sense of the rightness of normal marriage. Most often, by far, the agency of comic rebuke for the husband is the horned ridicule of cuckoldry—and the plays of the Restoration bear repeated witness to the never-ending application of this cruel comic therapy.

An awareness that the tragedy of *Othello* somehow transmutes the theme of comedy's attempt to achieve normal marriage provides, for what otherwise might seem a merely perverse opinion of Dr. Johnson, a context of justification:

> I observed [says Boswell], the great defect of the tragedy of *Othello* was, that it had not a moral; for that no man could resist the circumstances of suspicion which were artfully suggested to Othello's mind. JOHNSON. "In the first place, Sir, we learn from *Othello* this very useful moral, not to make an unequal match. . . ."

Focused by Johnson's strong-minded and unorthodox insight are, on the one hand, the foundation motif of comedy—society's preoccupation not only with the control of sex through marriage, but with the normalization of marriage itself through standards of propriety—and on the other, a recognition that by his marriage Othello has, from such a normative standpoint, committed an error. Much the same sense of the pertinence of comic matrices for the central relationship of the tragedy gleams through Rymer's impatient dismissal of its action as "plainly none other than a Bloody Farce," or through his sarcastic suggestion that it "may be a caution to all Maidens of Quality how, without their Parents consent, they run away with Blackamoors." And it is true, we realize upon reflection, that all the features of Othello's wedding, from the standpoint of social fittingness, are wrong. His difference in color from Desdemona is a dramatic emblem of social incompatibility (the fact that "I am black" is his first reflection when he ponders the possibility that Desdemona is "gone" [III.iii.263–7]); the elopement is an evasion of the ritual by which a wedding is socially accepted; the lack of parental consent is a portent of trouble ("Look to her, Moor, if thou hast eyes to see;/ She has deceiv'd her father, and may thee" [I.iii.293–4]). Above all, the difference in age, with its concomitant indication of difference in sexual need, is emphasized by the play. "It cannot be long," muses Iago, from outside the reality of love, but with a practiced eye for the probabilities of life, "that Desdemona should continue her love to the Moor. . . . She must change for youth; when she is sated with his body, she will find the error of her choice" (I.iii.347–57). And such a conjecture seems to accord with the implications of Othello's own moving, but noticeably not passionate, description of the basis of their marriage: "She lov'd me for the dangers I had pass'd,/ And I lov'd her that she did pity them" (I.iii.167–8). Moreover, when tormented by doubt, Othello himself says "Haply . . . for I am declin'd/ Into the vale of years,—yet that's not much—/ She's gone" (III.iii.263–7). Othello, in short, is literally old

enough to be Desdemona's father. Not only does Brabantio's "She has deceiv'd her father, and may thee"
suggest the Moor's position as father surrogate instead
of ideal husband, but Brabantio's extreme reaction to his
daughter's action, together with her own explicit rejection of father for husband:

> My noble father . . .
> . . . here's my husband;
> And so much duty as my mother show'd
> To you, preferring you before her father,
> So much I challenge that I may profess
> Due to the Moor, my lord.

> (I.iii.180–9)

further emphasizes, by its competitive alignment, the
mismatch in the ages of Othello and Desdemona. Most
of all, the social impropriety of their match is implied in
the initial circumstances of their meeting; for Othello is
the friend, and implied contemporary, not of Desdemona, but of her father:

> Her father lov'd me; oft invited me;
> Still question'd me the story of my life
> . . . These to hear
> Would Desdemona seriously incline;
> But still the house-affairs would draw her thence,
> Which ever as she could with haste dispatch,
> She'd come again, and with a greedy ear
> Devour up my discourse: which I observing,
> Took once a pliant hour, and found good means
> To draw from her a prayer of earnest heart
> That I would all my pilgrimage dilate
> . . . My story being done
> . . . She thank'd me,
> And bade me, if I had a friend that lov'd her,
> I should but teach him how to tell my story,

And that would woo her. Upon this hint I spake.

(I.iii.128–166)

In the social fact of the mismatch of Othello and Desdemona, with its overtones of comic possibility, we find, accordingly, the ironic center of Othello's tragedy. For it is Othello's convulsive thrusting out from the expectations of society and the typings of comedy that hurls him into his terrifying and pitiable mistake. Comedy sees event from a social perspective—we laugh with our fellows, contagiously, as members of an audience, but that at which we laugh becomes thereby that from which we dissociate ourselves. We laugh at the atypical or socially unexpected, whether the object be a soldier who proves a coward, a lawmaker revealed as a fraud, a doctor unmasked as a quack, or any of the other familiar objects of comic ridicule; but our laughter is always a kind of destruction of the threat posed by any manifestation that, standing apart from the norm and mean of society, thereby exists as potential criticism of that norm. Laughter, as we all can attest from private experience, is potentially cruel in its use, and only our lack of identification with the objects of our derision prevents us from seeing its cruelty more vividly than we do. We laugh at the cuckolded carpenter of *The Miller's Tale* and approve the lusty deceptions of Alisoun and Nicholas, but were we ourselves the carpenter, then, we all know, laughter could not be our response. For when we see a situation, not as a predictable or typical instance of a general rule, but from within, as the events of a unique existence, at that moment we pass into the arena of tragedy.

Such a transformation is epitomized in the character of Brabantio. Initially he is presented from the mocking social perspective of foolish and doting father—his frantic interruptions, extravagant charges, and near-ludicrous language ("She is abus'd, stol'n from me, and

corrupted/ By spells and medicines . . ." [I.iii.60–1]),
particularly as contrasted to Othello's calm deportment,
strengthen such a view. His reaction, however, to his
daughter's statement of intent to remain with Othello,
takes on enormous dignity and at the same time changes
Brabantio from the comic type of foolish father to a
human being unique in his hurt:

> God be with you! I have done.
> Please it your Grace, on to the state-affairs.
> I had rather to adopt a child than get it.
> Come hither, Moor.
> I here do give thee that with all my heart
> Which, but thou hast already, with all my heart
> I would keep from thee. For your sake, jewel,
> I am glad at soul I have no other child;
> For thy escape would teach me tyranny,
> To hang clogs on them. I have done, my lord.
>
> (I.iii.189–98)

When Brabantio then replies to the Duke's social bro-
mides ("To mourn a mischief that is past and gone/ Is
the next way to draw new mischief on. . . . The robb'd
that smiles steals something from the thief") with the
sardonic "So let the Turk of Cyprus us beguile;/ We lose
it not, so long as we can smile./ He bears the sentence
well that nothing bears . . ." (I.iii.204–5, 208, 210–12);
he both rejects the Duke's attempt to cast him into
another social typing and insists on the uniqueness of his
pain. It is such a transformation that prepares us for the
fact, not socially probable, but tragically real, of Brabantio's death: "Poor Desdemon!" says Gratiano, "I
am glad thy father's dead./ Thy match was mortal to
him, and pure grief/ Shore his old thread in twain"
(V.ii.204–6). Comic fathers do not find the matches of
their daughters mortal; their grief shears no thread of life
in twain. Brabantio, in his immense vividness and

poignance—he is surely among the most intensely realized of all minor characters in Shakespeare—thus draws our attention to that change in attitude toward a figure that can move him from comic generality to tragic uniqueness.

In the same way, an intellectual, as a type, in the guise, say, of the indecisive or absent-minded professor, elicits our ridicule: we would, if we could, ridicule Hamlet. But we are prevented from ridiculing Hamlet by that change in perspective, moving from the typical to the unique, from the social to the individual, which is one of the major distinctions between the comic and tragic cognizance of human event. When Hamlet becomes, not the type of the other-than-ourselves, but, in the here-and-now of his dramatic presentation, that unique individual, Hamlet, Prince of Denmark, then we are forced to see with his own eyes, to orient ourselves, as it were, to a world that exists only through him—and then his indecision becomes, not ridiculous, but agonizing. Comedy sees human action from the point of view of the group: people and their events are viewed statistically, in terms of probability and expectation and norm; while tragedy looks out from the eyes of the individual: existentially, in terms of the wonderful givenness, the uniqueness, of "my" situation. Only the sexual attraction, for instance, that can be socialized as marriage is trusted in terms of comedy; the attraction that, under the designation of romantic love, asserts its uniqueness, moves into the realm of tragedy (and indeed, partly to agree with De Rougemont, always seems to destine its protagonists for death). Only marriage can assuage the comic lovesickness of Orsino or Orlando, or still the wit combat of Berowne and Rosaline, but to Antony and Cleopatra marriage is irrelevant—their love is represented as an existentially unique event that cannot be assigned a place in the common life of the group.

The love of Othello and Desdemona, however, is neither the great passion of an Antony and Cleopatra, on the one hand, nor the socially applauded union of Beatrice and Benedick, on the other; it is rather a love caught in ironic ambivalence between its existential claim to unique dignity and its social identification as mismatch.

This ambivalence constitutes the irreducible irony of the play. Indeed, in largest statement, the perplexities of *Othello* might be seen as a progressive forcing of this basic irony through a sequence of tragic permutations. First of all, Othello, in marrying Desdemona, engages the comic theme of mismatch by the very action in which he asserts the existential wonder of his love. Then, when presented with the socially (comically) predictable pattern of his love—where the probabilities are that Desdemona is unfaithful and he himself a cuckold—he ferociously rejects the typed role for himself. But the act— the murder of Desdemona—by which he irrevocably asserts his existential control of his identity, ironically rejects the existential possibility that Desdemona might in fact, as opposed to probability, be faithful. "I do not think," said Coleridge in a statement that, though not wholly adequate, points us toward Othello's refusal to accept the *typing* of jealousy, "there is any jealousy, properly so called, in the character of Othello . . . he was not jealous, that is, of a jealous habit. . . ." Jealousy, as a human emotion reciprocal with the very possibility of love, Othello does indeed feel ("Then must you speak/ . . . Of one not easily jealous, but, being wrought/ Perplex'd in the extreme" [V.ii.343–6]); but jealousy as the comic affect of the superannuated husband—that character-mark of jealousy displayed by, say Jonson's Corvino, whose Celia, "a beauty ripe as harvest," is "kept as warily as is your gold;/ Never does come abroad, never takes air/ But at a windore," or by *The Changeling's* Alibius ("I am old, Lollio") who forever fears for his wife's faithfulness ("There's the fear, man;/ I would wear my ring on my own finger;/ Whilst it is borrowed, it is none of mine,")—such jealousy cannot, as Coleridge saw, be properly ascribed to the Moor, even though one of Iago's subtlest taunts is in fact to ascribe it. But Othello rejects the role of jealous husband:

> Think'st thou I'd make a life of jealousy,
> To follow still the changes of the moon
> With fresh suspicions? . . .
> . . . No, Iago;
> I'll see before I doubt; when I doubt, prove;
> And on the proof, there is no more but this,—
> Away at once with love or jealousy!
>
> (III.iii.177–92)

In such a refusal, Othello makes it repeatedly clear that he sees comic ridicule, which treats men as types, as the chief opponent of existential dignity. "Dost thou mock me?" he asks Iago, and when Iago, attempting to coax him into the type of the patient cuckold, responds, "Would you would bear your fortune like a man!" Othello savagely rejects the proffered comic identification: to Iago's "How is it, General? Have you not hurt your head?" he replies: "A horned man's a monster and a beast" (IV.i.60–3). From an existential standpoint, the dissolution of the individual in the norms and probabilities of the group falsifies existence—"das Man," the impersonal, social "one," and his ambiance of "durchschnittliche Alltäglichkeit," daily normality, are incompatible with authentic existence.

Again, Othello's great lament in the second scene of the fourth act is based on explicit recognition of the threat of comic typing: "but, alas, to make me/ The fixed figure for the time of scorn/ To point his slow unmoving finger at!" (IV.ii.53–5). Even in treating Desdemona as a whore, in denouncing her as "strumpet,"

Othello seems to be transferring to her the social typing that has been thrust upon him as "cuckold." But the excruciating irony in his assertion of existential uniqueness —his understanding of himself as exception to the type of the cuckold—is that he does not, by the same token, realize the existential uniqueness of Desdemona's love as exception to the probabilities of social mismatch.

The disharmonies of the play are forced through this sequence by a double impetus, supplied on the one hand by Iago, and on the other, by Othello himself. And both motive sources reveal themselves as drawing their dreadful power from the twisting of the existential possibility of unique event (Jaspers' "exception") against the probabilities of social norm. To realize to the fullest the ironies in the interaction of Othello and Iago is at the same time to remove the chief objection that has been leveled against the play: that it lacks plausibility. Not only was Rymer's attack based on this contention, but a substantial tradition, both of acting and commentary, has found itself unable to conceive both Othello and Iago in simultaneously satisfactory ways.

In briefest terms, the difficulty in accepting the interaction of the two figures seems to be that if Iago is conceived as a reasonably motivated character, Othello appears as simply stupid—as so opaque, indeed, that the special clarities of the tragic vision could not be attained from the perspective of his character. If, on the other hand, Othello is regarded as a figure of normal sagacity, then criticism has difficulty understanding the human logic of Iago's power to deceive him. The structure of this difficulty is dictated by the intense closeness of dramatic encounter between the two characters. "I am bound to thee for ever," says Othello to Iago (III.iii.213), and when, on a later occasion, he says to Iago, "Now art thou my lieutenant," the new lieutenant mockingly corrects the emphasis: "I am your own for ever" (III.iii.478–9). The bond is emphasized by the language of the play: "Were they as prime as goats, as hot as monkeys" leers Iago (III.iii.403), and Othello's dark muttering accordingly becomes "Goats and monkeys!" (IV.i.274). G. Wilson Knight, indeed, has elucidated the relationship as one almost of a single split personality, as one that hints at the alternate possibilities of nobility and degradation in any man; and at the very least, Iago echoes the morality tradition of the "badde aungel" attached to "mankynde," in the words of the banns to *The Castle of Perseverance,* to lead him "euere to hys dampnacion."

The implication of this closeness of the two characters is, for the critic, that it is not possible to settle on the interpretation of one role without settling also on the other, nor to adjust our understanding of either figure without corresponding adjustments in the other. It is not, furthermore, possible to have a plausible Iago and an implausible Othello, nor a plausible Othello and an implausible Iago. If the play leads us to tragic vision, it cannot violate the logic of our experience.

Now the defining irony of Iago's role as villain, like that of Othello's role as lover, consists in a tension between societal probability and existential possibility. It is by means of the common denominator supplied by this tension that we may resolve the seeming implausibility in the interaction of the two characters. Like Othello as lover, Iago as villain represents an existential exception. The fact is indicated by a special feature of the play's language: a semantic of diabolism that surrounds his utterance and description. He hates Othello "as I do hell-pains" (I.i.155). He celebrates the formulation of his plan in fiendish overtones: "I have't. It is engend'red. Hell and night/ Must bring this monstrous birth to the world's light" (I.iii.409–10). He apostrophizes, at the end of the second act, the

> Divinity of hell!
> When devils will the blackest sins put on,

> They do suggest at first with heavenly shows,
> As I do now
>
> (II.iii.356-9)

He speaks of "the spite of hell, the fiend's arch-mock" (IV.i.71); he notes that his suggestions "Burn like the mines of sulphur" (III.iii.329); he says that Brabantio is "one of those that will not serve God, if the devil bid you" (I.i.108-9). Such suggestive rays are focused by Othello's words at the end of the play: "I look down towards his feet; but that's a fable./ If that thou be'st a devil, I cannot kill thee" (V.ii.286-7). And then, tantalizingly in such a context, Othello is able only to wound Iago. Still further suggestion of theological overtone for Iago's evil is supplied by such teasing matter as his sardonic "O grace! O Heaven forgive me!" (III.iii.373) and his declaration, "I am not what I am" (I.i.65), which, in catching up the declaration of God as to his identity ("And God said unto Moses, I AM THAT I AM" [Exodus 3:14]), does so by way of total opposition.

Though such diabolistic overtones provide no license for an allegorizing of Iago, they do function in our consideration of the meaning of his role. They accord especially with the comic outline distortedly present behind the tragic marriage of Othello and Desdemona. For Iago's diabolism not only identifies him as the "badde aungel" attached to Othello, but, in his role as troublemaking plotter, makes of him a grotesque analogue of that most protean of comic bequests from the morality tradition: The Vice. The Vice, however, is, in the comic domain, always benign; and in his high efflorescence as a Sir Toby Belch or a Tony Lumpkin his characteristically demonic energy in troublemaking is accompanied by a truly enormous aura of benignity. Without enquiring into the history of the morality's transformation of the balefully threatening into the comically reassuring, we can, in short, realize that The Vice, the devil's messenger, is a tame demon. Where the conception of a true demon frightens, the comically blunted conception of the benignant Vice reassures. The diabolism of Iago ("a being," in Coleridge's insight, "next to devil, and only not quite devil") accords, therefore, with the comic paradigm that lies behind the play. But just as the marriage of Othello and Desdemona is twisted from comic type to tragic uniqueness, so the Vice-figure of Iago enters the tragedy of *Othello* as an agent of demonic malignity—as though the comic vaccine of the morality Vice were suddenly to be supplanted by the disease itself.

If Iago's diabolism affords him entrance to the comic possibility of the plot, it likewise functions in the tragic reality of that plot. For the dedication to hatred that characterizes Iago is unaccountable in probable terms: in modern psychological perspective we might indicate its exceptional quality by such a word as "psychopathic," while in common speech, as in theological usage, we might simply use the word "diabolical." Either word serves to indicate an evil action that has no immediately discernible motivation—no assignable antecedent cause whose probability of effect can be conceded by the group. Of such improbability is the action of Iago. Despite his statement, at the opening of the play, of a motive for hating Othello

> Three great ones of the city,
> In personal suit to make me his lieutenant,
> Off-capp'd to him . . .
> I know my price; I am worth no worse a place.
>   But he . . .
> Nonsuits my mediators; for, "Certes," says he,
> "I have already chose my officer."

> (I.i.8–17)

and not only despite, but because of, later statements of motivation, as

> I hate the Moor;
> And it is thought abroad that 'twixt my sheets
> He has done my office. I know not if't be true
> But I, for mere suspicion in that kind,
> Will do as if for surety
>
> (I.iii.392–6)

and again,

> I do suspect the lusty Moor
> Hath leap'd into my seat; the thought whereof
> Doth, like a poisonous mineral, gnaw my inwards;
> And nothing can or shall content my soul
> Till I am even'd with him, wife for wife.
>
> (II.i.304–8)

—despite such claims, Iago can be seen as having only one motivation for his actions: the improbable motive of uncaused hatred intertwined with generalized envy. Iago's stated reasons are not motives, but rationalizations. His self-justification, in Coleridge's key insight, is "the motive-hunting of a motiveless malignity."

The possibility of such special, seemingly unmotivated destructiveness is everywhere confirmed in our experience of the world, and we should be careful not to confuse its improbability with implausibility. The act of sudden violence by which a guard in a concentration camp beats to death the prisoner who may have survived numerous previous encounters testifies to the reality of "motiveless malignity." The hitchhiker who, in exception to the probabilities of the road, kills a man he does not even know, the discharged marine who slays a president, the father who murders his whole family—these, and other sad realities of daily report, are actions of evil that seem unmotivated to those most nearly concerned in their effect. Though for such action psychoanalysis can show conditioning psychic factors that may, in after-perspective, be seen as motivations from the past, such explanation circumvents the ordinary cause-and-effect understandings of social intercourse. And it likewise does not accord (unless, as is the case for *Hamlet,* the effect of the hidden past is part of the very fabric of meaning) with the conventions for the depiction of dramatic motivation. The past of Iago is notably inaccessible: he has "look'd upon the world for four times seven years," and the loveless condition of that time is hinted by its lesson of how to "distinguish betwixt a benefit and an injury" (I.iii.312–14); but the play directs us to the fact of his evil, not to an etiology that enlists our sympathy.

The statements of Iago, moreover, are everywhere suspect. "Reputation," he says to Cassio in one situation, "is an idle and most false imposition; oft got without merit, and lost without deserving" (II.iii.268–70); to Othello, however, in another situation, he says the direct opposite:

> Good name in man and woman, dear my lord,
> Is the immediate jewel of their souls
> . . . he that filches from me my good name
> Robs me of that which not enriches him,
> And makes me poor indeed.
>
> (III.iii.155–61)

Such dramatic indication of inconstant opinion serves to direct attention to a simple truth: Iago is, before all else, a liar. He renders homage to "Janus"—the two-faced god. (I.ii.33) But the lack of verifiability, as well as the disconcerting contradictoriness, that characterize his utterance throughout the play turn back upon him—as though, in misleading others, he is at the same time unclear about himself. He repeatedly makes statements, in soliloquy as well as in interlocution, that might be true in probability but are irrelevant to the particular situation, or, conversely, might be true in a particular situation, but do not cohere with other statements he makes. The net effect of all such idiosyncrasy is to impeach the reliability of his claims within the dramatic framework.

Now Kittredge, in opposition to Coleridge, attempts to see Iago's language as forthright, and Iago's motivation as therefore probable:

> It would be strange indeed if Iago, of all men, were left without a motive. . . . In fact, Iago's initial motive is set forth with passionate point. He is actuated by resentment for injustice, and there are few motives to which men so instantly respond. Cassio has the place which Iago expected and to which, so far as we can weigh their merits, he seems to have had the better claim. . . . There is no difficulty, then, in finding a motive for Iago, and . . . this motive is not only human (that is, neither monstrous nor maniacal), but has a kind of foundation in reason and justice. . . .

But it does not follow, in the probabilities of military life, that Iago, the practical soldier, is entitled to higher rank than Cassio, who is the imported specialist, trained in theory (". . . a great arithmetician,/ One Michael Cassio, a Florentine,/ . . . That never set a squadron in the field," says Iago, and notes that Cassio's experience is limited to "the bookish theoric" [I.i.19–24]). Not only does theoretical training, in almost any endeavor, command a higher place than practical experience, but the sergeant of twenty years experience, in all armies, has always, as the new-fledged lieutenant from the military academy is set over him, murmured that the fledgling "never set a squadron in the field,/ Nor the division of a battle knows/ . . . Mere prattle without practice/ Is all his soldiership" (I.i.22–7).

Yet it is not necessary to attempt an adjudication of the relative merits of Iago and Cassio as soldiers. Cassio has in fact been chosen, and the problem has to do with the appropriateness of Iago's response. Even if it be conceded that Iago actually deserved the lieutenancy, it hardly follows that his disappointment provides probable cause for his mortal assaults. Despite Kittredge's view that Iago's resentment has "a kind of foundation in reason and justice," neither law nor morality sanctions his actions. Almost every man, in the course of his years, expects to cope with analogous disappointments without resort to demonic retaliation. Iago concedes as much himself, when, a few lines later, he says to Roderigo in protean reversal: "Why, there's no remedy. 'Tis the curse of service,/ Preferment goes by letter and affection,/ And not by old gradation" (I.i.35–7).

Nor is Iago's conjecture of an affair between Othello and Emilia a motivation of sounder base. Not only does no whisper of such a possibility issue from any other character in the play, but the presented interactions of Othello and Emilia, particularly in view of the discrepancy of their sensibilities as revealed in their language, render the plausibility of such an affair almost null. And again, even if the affair itself were not implausible, Iago's statements and reactions about its hypothetical existence are exceedingly so. Any husband who cared—who was not merely searching out a pretext for action—would, before all else, have to exchange suspicion for knowledge. Iago's satisfaction with an indeterminate suspicion ("I know not if't be true") rings counterfeit against the psychological rightness of Othello's agonized need to know: "No, Iago;/ I'll see before I doubt; when I doubt, prove . . ." (III.iii.189–90); ". . . be sure thou prove my love a whore;/ Be sure of it. Give me the ocular proof" (III.iii.359–60). Such, surely, is the only form of reaction that indicates the depth of feeling and concern necessary as motive sufficient to an act of vengeance.

Iago's language, furthermore, is as contradictory as his psychological reactions are implausible. He thinks it probable, for instance, that "It cannot be long that Desdemona should continue her love to the Moor. . . .

She must change for youth" (I.iii.347–56), and the implication is that Othello's age lessens his sexual activity, an implication given more specific statement, in the ambiance of Iago's preoccupation with lust, by later reference to Othello's "weak function" (II.iii.354). But the same Iago, when hunting for motives, says, of the same Othello, "I do suspect the lusty Moor/ Hath leap'd into my seat" (II.i.304–5). If Iago cannot conceive Othello as satisfying Desdemona, he can hardly, with any credit, conceive him as then possessing the residual powers necessary to validate the charge that "the lusty Moor/ Hath leap'd into my seat."

The plausibility of Iago's statements as motivation is still further impeached—and, inversely, their nature as rationalization authenticated—by their random proliferation. Iago suggests, in his opening speech to Roderigo, that ambition for status makes him want to destroy Othello; but later he also wants, for the same reason, to destroy Cassio. And to the service of this branching direction of hate, he again insouciantly applies—in a way that weakens its potential validity in either case—the suspicion of Emilia's infidelity ("For I fear Cassio with my night-cap too" [II.i.316]). He says, still again, that he is impelled by a competitive love of Desdemona ("Now, I do love her too" [II.i.300]). But elsewhere he says "love" is "merely a lust of the blood and permission of the will," and that "we have reason to cool our raging motions; our carnal stings, our unbitted lusts" (I.iii.334–6)—to which may be added his contemptuous words that scoff at Roderigo's proposal to drown himself for "the love of a guinea-hen" (I.iii.316–17).

Thus, Iago has none of the probable motivations credited by society. Just as the comic Vice always seems to draw his ebullient energies from his character alone, rather than from the circumstances of the plot, so Iago's hatred flows out of him as from a fountain of hidden source. Even before the play opens, he has established his hate: "Thou told'st me," says Roderigo, "thou didst hold him in thy hate" (I.i.6)—and the vagueness of the pronoun "him," which has no antecedent, concentrates emphasis on the given and primordial fact of this hatred. Iago's is a kind of idealism of hatred, a twisted altruism that reveals itself as the dark shadow of love, and that leads him to pursue his ends with a dedication that rises above personal risk. The motivations Iago searches for are affects of, rather than causes of, that hate: "Now, sir," he asks in an almost plaintive request for confirmation, "be judge yourself/ Whether I in any just term am affin'd/ To love the Moor" (I.i.38–40). "I had told thee often," he says again to Roderigo, "and I re-tell thee again and again, I hate the Moor" (I.iii.372–3). "I hate the Moor . . . ," he says (I.iii.392); "I endure him not . . ." (II.i.297); "I do hate him . . ." (I.i.155).

This pure, inexplicable hatred, of transcendent origin, whose analogies we find, in diminished form, in the unbidden envies of our own lives, and whose unaccountability we recognize, in philosophical perspective, as an adjunct of its universal possibility, is the key not only to the meaning of Iago's action, but to his ability to function unsuspected by Othello. That Othello does not detect the hatred of Iago is the result of the improbability of that hatred. Othello's unawareness of its presence stems, not from a lack of sagacity, but from a habitual commitment to the interlocked consequences of probability in a world whose motivations are the "sole self-good" that Mendoza the Machiavel identifies as the only valid motive to action. In his commitment to the probabilities and predictabilities of human participation in the large events of the world, Othello does not allow for existential exception—the self-sacrifice of the man who hates only because he hates.

This unawareness of Othello to the motivation of Iago not only constitutes the most urgent witness of all to the improbability of that motivation in its true nature, but is twisted into special irony by an inescapable emphasis of Othello's character as posited by his situation. If Othello has in fact unfairly blocked Iago's career, or done him the wrong of cuckoldry, then surely his lack of watchfulness toward Iago becomes wholly implausible, even in a man of slow wits and small knowledge of the world—and the human logic of the play collapses. But the human logic of the play cannot be impeached; Othello's lack of suspicion toward Iago is dictated, not by stupidity, but by a special knowingness, an economy of attention that is the mark of those experienced in the world. Toward probable motives—ambition, fear, greed, and other avatars of self-interest—the worldly man is keenly alert; and Othello is presented, not only as a worldly man, but as that man whose irreducible characteristic is not to trust, as that man skilled in looking below the surface of flattery to see the universal motives of self-interest hidden there—as, in short, the man of Machiavellian commitments. For whatever we make of Iago's statement that "The Moor is of a free and open nature,/ That thinks men honest that but seem to be so" (I.iii.405–6) —perhaps we should here recall Coleridge's admonition that "it is a common error to mistake the epithets applied by the *dramatis personae* to each other, as truly descriptive of what the audience ought to see or know"—whatever we make of Iago's statement, and however much Othello's worldly aspiration may give place, in the situation of the play, to his emotional perplexities, the Moor is, in the unavoidable implications of his past activity, as indicated by his present public position, necessarily and precisely a Machiavellian figure. He is the man whose competence in the world is hailed by worldlings—the man "whom our full Senate/ Call all in all sufficient" (IV.i.275–6). Indeed, in this regard even the statement that seems most drastically to limit Othello's worldly wisdom—that is, his own willingness to restrict his claims of competence to military matters ("And little of this great world can I speak/ More than pertains to feats of broils and battle" [I.iii.86–7])—actually serves to authenticate his Machiavellianism. For "A Prince"— as Machiavelli himself insists in a climactic statement— "ought to have no other ayme, nor other thought, nor take any thing else for his proper arte, but warr, and the orders and discipline thereof."

And not only as a power figure in the flux of worldly events does Othello activate the Machiavellian ethos, but, in ironic fact, he stands, of all the Machiavel figures projected by Shakespeare, closest to the actual historical paradigm supplied by Machiavelli: that is, the Machiavel as commander of the military forces of a city-state in Renaissance Italy. The setting of the play—in time, place, and context of activity—invites comparison of Othello to the man of power in whose eulogy *The Prince* was composed: to Cesare Borgia, commander of the military forces of Rome. And it invites comparison also to such ruthless and devious compeers as Sigismondo Malatesta of Rimini, or Lodovico Sforza, the Moor of Milan. Indeed, Othello's role as an outsider, as a black man in a group of white men, as a foreigner in Venetian society, emphasizes his competence in the world of power. Even a Cesare Borgia was a duke, as well as the son of a pope, but Othello has attained his position by aid neither of family nor of title.

Moreover, that same declination into "the vale of years" that causes him concern in his marriage is, in the perspective of Machiavellian achievement, the guarantee of the fullness of his experience in the ways of the world —an experience not, significantly, of books and theories of human behavior, but of the real actions of men. Though he skillfully disclaims, to the senate, any worldly knowledge ("And little of this great world can I speak"), the disclaimer is a litotes that prepares the way for our realization of the enormous range of his experience: ". . . the story of my life" consists of "most disastrous

chances,/ Of moving accidents by flood and field," of—
and here, surely, one would gain education in the baseness of human possibilities—"being taken by the insolent
foe/ And sold to slavery," of the "portance in my travel's
history," which, in its geographical extensiveness ("of
antres vast and deserts idle,/ Rough quarries, rocks, and
hills whose heads touch heaven") is a warrant of varie-
gated observations of the types and customs, and fear-
some possibilities, of mankind (". . . of the Cannibals that
each other eat,/ The Anthropophagi, and men whose
heads/ Do grow beneath their shoulders"). His "youth"
has "suffer'd" many a "distressful stroke"; his existence is remarkable for "the dangers I had pass'd"
(I.iii.86–167).

. Such a man cannot be conceived as wholly insensitive
to the baser motivations of human action. The man of
power is surrounded—to cite Jonson's *Sejanus*—by
"shift of faces" and "cleft of tongues," by men who "can
lie,/ Flatter, and swear, forswear, deprave, inform,/
Smile, and betray," and there is no reason to think Iago
any more adept in such wiles ("not I for love and duty,"
he says, "But seeming so, for my peculiar end"
[I.i.59–60]) than other aspirants to power. Nor is there
reason to think Othello uninformed as to the ways in
which to deal with those striving to dislodge him from
his eminence. His option is not merely that of sudden
violence—the instant murder ("Before he casts a plot")
of *The Malcontent*—but is, as well, that "trick of state"
which "jealous princes never fail to use" that is recom-
mended in *Sejanus* as a means to "decline that growth"
of competitive subordinates: "with fair pretext,/ And
honorable colors of employment/ . . . To shift them forth
into another air/ Where they may purge and lessen."

Othello, in brief, must be conceived as a more subtle,
sagacious, experienced, and deadly man—a more wary,
suspicious, and sudden man than previous criticism has
usually been prepared to grant. Talking with "honest

Iago," seemingly oblivious to all but his agony of sur-
mise, suddenly he turns, and with no apparent cause for
suspicion, breathes lethally near the truth: "Villain, be
sure thou prove my love a whore;/ Be sure of it"
(III.iii.359–60). Such words indicate that Iago's plan
involves dangers as deadly for himself, in the realm of
possibility, as they do for his victims; and they ill accord
with his ascription of a "free and open nature" to the
Moor.

But these truths of Othello's character are explicitly
focused, and thereby reveal new meaning, by an inspection of his reaction toward the possible truth of the
charges against Desdemona. In that reaction, we nowhere see any "free and open nature" in the Moor, any
inclination "to think men honest." On the contrary,
Othello here displays character traits of sharp alertness
and extreme suspiciousness. From Iago's initial innu-
endo ("Ha! I like not that" [III.iii.35]), the play requires
less than two hundred virtuoso lines for the Moor to
reach a tormented paroxysm of jealousy—to reach, in
fact, the very verge of psychic collapse. "Othello has
from the beginning," says Leavis,

> responded to Iago's "communications" . . . with a
> promptness that couldn't be improved upon. . . . And
> it is plain that what we should see in Iago's prompt suc-
> cess is not so much Iago's diabolic intellect as Othello's
> readiness to respond. Iago's power, in fact, in the
> temptation-scene is that he represents something that is
> in Othello.

The insight is just. Othello takes up Iago's suggestion
with almost frightening alacrity. If the Moor, as he says
of himself, is "not easily jealous," then such speed of
acceptance implies that the major portion of jealousy's
work has already been done, that an emotional attitude
of tense and suspicious expectation exists in Othello before the advent of Iago's manipulations. Othello's atti-

tude, in other words, is fraught with anxiety. And on his anxiety depends the final ironic coherence in the human logic of his action.

Now anxiety is tenseness prior to the fact of specified threat, a gnawing anticipation of harm. "Das Wovor der Angst," says Heidegger, "ist völlig unbestimmt"—the object of anxiety is completely indefinite. Yet the greater our experience in the world, the more do we learn to anticipate dangers. Hence Heidegger, in a variant formulation, says "Das Wovor der Angst ist das In-der-Welt-sein als solches"—the object of anxiety is the simple fact of being in the world. A man declined, like Othello, into the "vale of years" feels anxieties not known by the man of once-and-twenty. A man with the lonely responsibilities of military command is more anxious than a man in the comforting anonymity of the ranks. Those very specifics, in brief, that mark Othello out as a man of uncommon achievement mark him out as a man burdened by uncommon anxiety: his blackness in a white society is not only a guarantee of his competence, but a visual symbol of his alienation and estrangement. His age is not only a guarantee of sagacity, but an index of the dissipation of vitality and of a moving toward death. The exotic specialness of his background signalizes his pride of individuality, but also his disjunction from the group. "That handkerchief," he says, "Did an Egyptian to my mother give;/ She was a charmer, and could almost read/ The thoughts of people. . . ./ . . . there's magic in the web of it" (III.iv.55–69).

All such experience—alienation, estrangement, dissipation of vitality, the growing awareness of death—constitutes a doorway to anxiety at the same time that it is inseparable from the very competences that set a man as leader above the group—"Die Angst," says Heidegger, "vereinzelt und erschliesst so das Dasein als 'solus ipse' " —anxiety isolates and reveals existence in its uniqueness.

The ambivalence is the very stuff of Othello's dramatic character. With less anxiety, he would be less vulnerable to Iago's suggestion; but with less anxiety he would not be Othello.

But the ironies ramify still further. As anxiety is generated by looking forward to no threat in particular, it is also generated by looking backward to the specific realizations of past experience. A child who has been burned not only dreads the fire but becomes more apprehensive in general. The same worldly experience that increases Othello's anxiety leads him to accept the probability that the marriage of a young woman of one race and milieu to an older man of another is indeed a mismatch. The more extensive a man's experience in human nature, the more the probabilities of its baseness impress themselves upon his anticipation. "O, wonder!" says Miranda, "How many goodly creatures are there here!/ How beauteous mankind is!"—but such a view is the opinion of youth and inexperience, of those to whom the world is brave and new. The true attributes of the group indicated by Miranda's rapture are, we know, disloyalty, selfishness, greed, and a lust for power. Thus Othello is whipsawed between two variations of possibility—the improbability of Iago's motivation leads the Moor to misplaced trust, while the probability of Desdemona's unfaithfulness, added to that trust, impels him to misdirected and ruinous action.

His own character is predicated upon exception; his hopes for his marriage with Desdemona are also predicated upon exception. Despite his knowledge of the probabilities of social mismatch, he enters the marriage in the hope of unique event. His proud statement, "For she had eyes, and chose me" (III.iii.189), not only takes into account the probabilities of mismatch—age, color, and the rest—but asserts the wonder of the visually real against the hypothetical nature of probability. Against the background of exception and wonderful event supplied by the deliverance of his ship from the storm, Othello greets his wife in noble serenity, free from the anxiety generated by the world of probabilities:

> It gives me wonder great as my content
> To see you here before me. O my soul's joy!
> If after every tempest come such calms,
> May the winds blow till they have waken'd death!
>
> (II.i.185–88)

But against the background of societal probabilities invoked by Iago's claim that he knows "our country disposition well;/ In Venice they do let Heaven see the pranks/ They dare not show their husbands" (III.iii.-201–3)—against such a background Othello's "content so absolute" (II.i.193) dissipates into his normal anxiety, and is transformed to the croaking rage of "I'll tear her all to pieces" (III.iii.431). The entire play devolves from these dreadful tensions between the societal realm of probability and the existential realm of unique event. "Put out the light," says Othello in one of the tragedy's greatest moments—and in referring to the taper in his hand he refers to the world of repetitions and probabilities—"and then put out the light"—and in referring to the light of Desdemona's life he invokes the great oneness, the uniqueness and the wonder, of human existence:

> If I quench thee, thou flaming minister,
> I can again thy former light restore,
> Should I repent me; but once put out thy light,
> Thou cunning'st pattern of excelling nature,
> I know not where is that Promethean heat
> That can thy light relume.
>
> (V.ii.7–13)

In dreadful irony Othello substitutes, for the unique event of the love for which he hoped, the unique event by which is quenched the light that human hands cannot restore.

It is not, therefore, solely by Iago's hate that Othello's vision is darkened, but also by the inner anxiety that arises from eroding repetitions of years and experience. In accepting the probability of Desdemona's unfaithfulness, Othello shows himself, ironically, worldly-wise rather than opaquely foolish. And the ironies compound. Where Othello's ignorance about his wife depends, not on doltish unawareness, but on too full a knowingness about general human nature, his wife's ignorance about him, in converse poignance, is precisely a total unawareness of that nature and its probabilities: "Dost thou in conscience think,—tell me, Emilia,—/ That there be women do abuse their husbands/ In such gross kind?" (IV.iii.61–3). Emilia, from her age and experience, responds, in protective diminution: "There be some such, no question." (IV.iii.63) But when Desdemona presses the point with "Wouldst thou do such a deed for all the world?" Emilia's attitude changes to one of surprise, and thereby accepts the very probabilities accepted by Othello: "Why, would not you?" The world, as Emilia says, with the respect engendered by experience, is "a huge thing; it is a great price/For a small vice" (IV.iii.-69–70). Desdemona's virtuous purity is not only an existentially unique event, but a youthful idealism and unawareness of the exceeding worldliness of the world. "In troth, I think thou wouldst not," she says, and Emilia, only half-joking, and quite firm, replies, "In troth, I think I should" (IV.iii.70–71). "I do not think there is any such woman," says Desdemona, as new as Miranda. "Yes, a dozen," responds Emilia drily (IV.iii.84–5).

Thus throughout the horrible sequence of interviews between Othello and Desdemona, Desdemona's unawareness of the probability of the situation ironically interlocks with Othello's too-knowing acceptance of that probability. Almost from the first of the play, in fact, Desdemona's innocent words, often mere girlish chatter, assume—in the matrix of probabilities we posit for Othello's experience and also acknowledge in our own—the status of damning evidence against her.

In such manner do chance, malice, and the inadequacy of human knowledge unite against the Moor. Given the decisiveness of Othello's character—without which, after all, he could not be seen as rising to his worldly eminence—; given the habit of violence—without which he would not be a soldier—; given the sense of existential exception in which resides all his dignity—: given all these factors, Othello's mortal swiftness logically follows his conviction of Desdemona's unfaithfulness.

Yet the irony is twisted tighter by Othello's care in attempting to ascertain the truth. His action is not precipitate, though it is quick and decisive. One of Rymer's sarcastic "Morals" to be derived from the play is that "This may be a lesson to Husbands that before their Jealousie be Tragical the proofs may be Mathematical." But, as the proverb says, seeing is believing. Othello's insistence that he be given "ocular proof" not only constitutes the most scrupulous kind of enquiry but, in painful irony, seeks to base knowledge of Desdemona's innocence on the same foundation as his hope for the love itself: "For she had eyes, and chose me. No, Iago;/ I'll see before I doubt" (III.iii.189–90). Given the will to falsification, even "Mathematical" proofs might deceive; ocular proof, Rymer notwithstanding, is proof of the highest order. Indeed, when much the same situation occurs in *Much Ado,* ocular proof convinces not one, but two witnesses. To discredit Hero with Claudio, Don John arranges "ocular" proof of Hero's infidelity: "I have tonight woo'd Margaret the Lady Hero's gentlewoman, by the name of Hero," says Don John's man

Borachio—"She leans me out at her mistress' chamber-window. . . . I should first tell thee how the Prince [and] Claudio . . . saw afar off in the orchard this amiable encounter." Here, as in *Othello,* such proof is considered valid, and in this case tragedy is averted only by the comic twist of the plot. The desire of human beings to know, as Aristotle says, makes them prefer sight to all other senses *(Metaphysics* 980^{a}22–28). Ocular proof, in drama as in life, may deceive, but when it does, in those matters where we depend on it, then we are powerfully thrust against the disharmony, futility, and tragic absurdity of our existence.

Of such ironic mixture is the brine that Othello, thirsting for love and righteousness, must drink to the lees. The draught is bitter, not only for him, but for all who move in the dank and trampling confines of the play—as well as for those who partake of it from theater or study. The vortex movement seems remorseless: horrible as it is to contemplate Othello as he mistakenly prepares to kill Desdemona, even more horrible is the fact that Desdemona does not accept death with the composure of dramatic convention, but pleads for life as though she were alive. After the murder, she lingers, and this torment is followed by an awful moment of shame in which Othello denies knowledge of his deed ("Why, how should she be murder'd. . . . You hear her say herself, it was not I" [V.ii.126–7]). And Othello—even violence failing him—is unable, not once, but twice, to kill Iago.

Thus does the play, in painful convolution, near its very end. But then there rises, from the dregs of its testimony of human perplexity, a fountain of life-giving language. As Othello begins, "Soft you; a word or two before you go," the first lie told by Iago falls away, and we realize the Moor's utterance has never been "bombast circumstance/ Horribly stuff'd with epithets of war" (I.i.13–14). The limpid truth continues:

> I have done the state some service, and they know't.
> No more of that. I pray you, in your letters,
> When you shall these unlucky deeds relate,
> Speak of me as I am; nothing extenuate,
> Nor set down aught in malice.

And as measured dignity lengthens to the cadence and language of final summation, the poison begins to clear from the wellspring of life:

> Then must you speak
> Of one that lov'd not wisely but too well;
> Of one not easily jealous, but being wrought,
> Perplex'd in the extreme; of one whose hand,
> Like the base Indian, threw a pearl away
> Richer than all his tribe;

—the words, now bright with longing, course toward an Eastern garden—

> of one whose subdu'd eyes
> Albeit unused to the melting mood,
> Drops tears as fast as the Arabian trees
> Their medicinable gum.

> (V.ii.338–51)

The sublime lie of the dying Desdemona (V.ii.124–5) finds its justification in the sublime truth of Othello's vision washed clean, and in his second swiftly mortal action, which wipes the tears forever from his eyes. The effects of a demonic hatred have perplexed the understanding and destroyed happiness, but still the spirit shines forth, unimpaired. For now Othello, though dark of fortune, reveals, at last and forever, that he is "great of heart" (V.ii.361).

Antony and Octavius*

Antony *and Cleopatra* presents us not only with a dramatic action but with a question, and an answer, about final concerns of the human situation. The question the tragedy poses may be described as a form of a problem that occupies philosophy and religion as well as art: What is the locus of reality? To use another phrasing, the play asks: In what does true existence consist?

The terms of the dramatic discourse that embody both question and answer were defined first and most clearly by Dryden, who named his rewriting of Shakespeare's titanic work *All for Love* and subtitled it, *Or, The World Well Lost*. In this basic formulation are revealed the two mighty opposites of *Antony and Cleopatra:* love and the world. Love and the World, striding forth al-

* This chapter first appeared as an article in the *Yale Review* (Winter, 1959). Copyright 1959 by the Yale University Press. By permission of the publisher.

most like personifications from an old morality play, contend in Antony's mind for dominion. With added dimensions, transfigured into the love of Antony and Cleopatra, and the world of Octavius, the struggle breaks from every point in Shakespeare's pattern; and when this pattern imprints its form on the stuff of our own life experience, the struggle, ever renewed, finds in each of us its counterpart.

The opposition of love and the world is defined in the opening speech of the play, where Philo bids Demetrius take note of Antony's entrance:

> Take but good note, and you shall see in him
> The triple pillar of the world transform'd
> Into a strumpet's fool.

$$(\text{I.i.11–13})$$

The description sets the situation at the beginning of the play. The world is viewed as virtue, the love of Antony and Cleopatra as lust. Philo's choric opinion is precisely that stated later by the world's protagonist, Octavius Caesar, who in Act Three says that Antony "hath given his empire/ Up to a whore" (III.vi.66–7). In both opinions the world is viewed honorifically—by Philo as a proud structure raised on the shoulders of mighty Atlases, by Octavius as an empire. And in both opinions love is not only denigrated, but more significantly, treated as non-existent: to Philo, Cleopatra is a strumpet, to Octavius, a whore, and, presumably to both, Antony is a fool. The play begins, therefore, with the world in the moral ascendant, with love regarded as foolishness, or lust, or, as Philo says, as "dotage." Antony's "captain's heart . . . is become the bellows and the fan/ To cool a gipsy's lust" (I.i.6–10).

The first appearance of Antony and Cleopatra reinforces the sense of the situation conveyed by Philo's speech. We see Cleopatra, a woman of uncertain temper and uncertain age, worrying the attachment, captiously demanding an exact accounting of Antony's love: "If it be love indeed, tell me how much." And her introduction of the word "if" lends fearful credence to Philo's and the world's forthright denunciation of the relationship as simple lust. Antony's reply, "There's beggary in the love that can be reckon'd," displays, perhaps, a healthier realization, but his use of the word "beggary" introduces the tone of bankruptcy that permeates the entire first act: the moral bankruptcy of Egypt as opposed to the virtue of Rome, the near-bankruptcy of the relationship of Antony and Cleopatra as opposed to the call of Antony's duties in the great world.

The intrusion of the messenger—the agent of the world's business—launches Cleopatra into a graceless, hoydenish denunciation of Antony's wavering:

> Nay, hear them, Antony.
> Fulvia perchance is angry; or, who knows
> If the scarce-bearded Caesar have not sent
> His powerful mandate to you: "Do this, or this;
> Take in that kingdom, and enfranchise that"
>
> (I.i.19–23)

Her very manner is unlovable, and lends irony to the vague and automatic answer of Antony: "How, my love?" She shrills again, and Antony, revealing himself for the first time, states the terms of the great opposition, the world versus love:

> Let Rome in Tiber melt, and the wide arch
> Of the rang'd empire fall! Here is my space.
> Kingdoms are clay. . . .
> . . . the nobleness of life
> Is to do thus,

and as he says "thus," he embraces Cleopatra:

>   when such a mutual pair
> And such a twain can do't . . .

The world to weet we stand up peerless.

(I.i.33–40)

The statement re-echoes: "Let Rome in Tiber melt," "Kingdoms are clay"—the world is dismissed. In love alone lies true existence—"Here is my space," "The nobleness of life is to do thus." The words of Philo are momentarily submerged under the flood of Antony's emotion and conviction. But the sense of impermanence, the feeling of bankruptcy, of weariness, reappears immediately. To Antony's speech Cleopatra whispers crushingly: "Excellent falsehood," and, almost agreeing with Philo, adds in a malicious aside: "I'll seem the fool I am not.—Antony/ Will be himself" (I.i.40–43).

The second scene of the first act widens and intensifies the situation presented in the first scene. Not only the love of Antony and Cleopatra, but Egypt itself, is revealed as on the brink of moral bankruptcy, lushly corrupt, luxurious, lecherous, and, most damning of all, mindless. "O excellent!" says Charmian, "I love long life better than figs" (I.ii.32), and the wonderfully mindless triviality of the line epitomizes the whole aura of the Egyptian court—epitomizes the trivial present, and in addition prepares for the future sublimities the play is to unfold. Charmian's dalliance with life is matched by the choric cynicism of the Roman Enobarbus: "Mine, and most of our fortunes to-night, shall be—drunk to bed" (I.ii.45–46). Into this picture of aimless non-existence obtrudes once more the demands of the world, in the guise of a second messenger, with further news of the empire. And Antony now shows himself wavering in the face of the seeming moral ascendency of the world and its demands: duty, honor, responsibility. "These strong Egyptian fetters I must break," he says, speaking in the accents of a worldly Roman, with the Roman's disdain for luxurious Egypt, "Or lose myself in dotage" (I.ii.-120–21). And his acceptance of the choric view of the spiritual superiority of the world is emphasized by his use of the word "dotage," for "dotage" was the opening noun of the play.

Significantly, the play stresses again, immediately, Antony's ebbing emotion, his feeling of the unreality in his relationship with Cleopatra, of the reality in the claims of the world. The messenger from Sicyon brings news of Fulvia's death, and Antony, shaken, exclaims: "I must from this enchanting queen break off;/ Ten thousand harms, more than the ills I know,/ My idleness doth hatch" (I.ii.132–34). The Roman fear of idleness, the Roman worship of worldly responsibility, the Roman blindness to love, revealed in Antony's denial of the reality of his love for Cleopatra, constitute the low point of his stature in the play, and the specific Romanness of such sentiment is brutally emphasized by the speech of Enobarbus that immediately follows: "Under a compelling occasion, let women die," says Enobarbus—the "die" pun coarsely highlighting the Roman view of love as lust—and then, placing himself fully with the world against love, he adds: "It were pity to cast [women] away for nothing; though, between them and a great cause, they should be esteemed nothing" (I.ii.141–44). With Enobarbus's speech we realize, for the first time, the irrevocable nature of the opposition: the choice must be either the world or love; never, under any final circumstances, may one have both the world and love. If the world truly exists, then human relationships are to be "esteemed nothing."

Lubriciously, Enobarbus continues:

Cleopatra, catching but the least noise of this, dies instantly; I have seen her die twenty times upon far poorer moment.   (I.ii.144–47)

Antony, bemused, responds with a statement that foreshadows in Cleopatra far more than the play has yet revealed of her character: "She is cunning past man's thought" (I.ii.150). Shortly afterward, at the beginning of the third scene, we are made more concretely aware of the thinkingness of Cleopatra. Hitherto we have seen her merely as an aging woman, utilizing all her formidable arsenal of wiles in a dreary attempt to keep Antony interested by keeping him off balance. "See where he is, who's with him, what he does," she commands Charmian, "If you find him sad,/ Say I am dancing; if in mirth, report/ That I am sudden sick" (I.iii.2–5). When Charmian interposes an objection, and counsels that Cleopatra should "In each thing give him way, cross him in nothing," there flashes from Cleopatra something harder than we have yet seen: "Thou teachest like a fool: the way to lose him" (I.iii.9–10). We see her character. To her the relationship is too important to be trusted to emotion alone; intellect, calculation, all the force of her being, are turned to its preservation. And still we have not seen why. The opinion of the world concerning the love of Antony and Cleopatra has not been impeached; sensuality, daily more jaded, seems to be the sole chain that binds them together or has bound them together in the past. And then Antony enters. Cleopatra announces that she is "sick and sullen" and behaves in a way to justify the claim. She upbraids Antony, logically and with at least seeming cause:

> Why should I think you can be mine and true,
> Though you in swearing shake the throned gods,
> Who have been false to Fulvia?

> (I.iii.27–29)

Antony's stumbling rejoiner: "Most sweet queen—" is cut off as Cleopatra returns to the attack:

> Nay, pray you, seek no colour for your going,
> But bid farewell and go.

> (I.iii.31–33)

And then, suddenly, there flames out from the play a statement of grandeur: "Eternity was in our lips and eyes." The words transmute for us the seemingly exhausted attachment of the tired warrior and the aging queen. "When you sued staying," says Cleopatra, "Then was the time for words; no going then;/ Eternity was in our lips and eyes,/ Bliss in our brows' bent; none our parts so poor/ But was a race of heaven" (I.iii.33–37). "Eternity was in our lips and eyes"—we encounter here for the first time the special radiance of language in which this play surpasses all others except *King Lear*. We experience for the first time the love of Antony and Cleopatra as that love is, not as the world sees it. We are seized by the apprehension that love is the locus of reality, that lovers are the truly existent. "By eternity," says Spinoza, "I mean existence itself." For the first time the world seems to have a fit antagonist.

And the realization is apparent in Antony's next speech. Gone are the tentative fumblings: "Now, my dearest queen—," "The gods best know—," "Cleopatra —." "Most sweet queen—," Instead a man speaks:

> Hear me, Queen.
> The strong necessity of time commands
> Our services awhile; but my full heart
> Remains in use with you.

> (I.iii.41–44)

If love partakes of eternity, then the world must involve eternity's opposite, "The strong necessity of time." But though time and the world exert their claim, eternity and love do not give way. Antony's "full heart/ Remains in use" with Cleopatra.

The fourth scene of the first act introduces the world's protagonist, Octavius Caesar. Throughout the play Octavius is the Machiavel, and we may define the Machiavel, then, now, in that play, in this life, as the man who treats the world as if it really exists. Alternatively, we may define the Machiavel by negative characteristic: he is the man who cannot love.

We meet the negative prescription at every turn of Octavius's devious course. He does not understand love, and because love cannot be communicated as knowledge, but can only be experienced as reality, he is unable to learn its nature. For him the reality of love truly does not exist, any more than to a man born, reared, and forever doomed to live in darkness, the reality of light could exist. For Octavius the good morrow has never dawned. Only as a word does love impinge upon his world, and he tries to cope with it by various formulae, trying first one description, then another. His first statement with regard to love is a negative one; though Caesar may not love, at least Caesar does not hate: "You may see, Lepidus, and henceforth know,/ It is not Caesar's natural vice to hate/ Our great competitor" (I.iv.1–3). His second statement is a sharper focusing of the controlling Roman attitude—love is lust: "Let is grant it is not/ Amiss to tumble on the bed of Ptolemy/ To give a kingdom for a mirth. . . ." (I.iv.16–18). And for lust no sane man would give a kingdom.

At this point in Octavius's initial complex of statements, a third definition of the Machiavel presents itself. The Machiavel, the man of policy, the man who plots, is the man who must live in the future. The very existence of his plans and strivings indicates that neither past nor present is bearable to him, and eternity is closed to him. So Octavius denounces the fact that Antony "confounds" the "time," and he says that Antony's conduct is "to be chid/ As we rate boys who, being mature in knowledge,/ Pawn their experience to their present pleasure" (I.iv.30–32). Maturity, for the Machiavel, is the willingness to pawn the present for the future, and Antony's unwillingness to do so brands him immature—a boy to be chid.

The charge is curious. Whatever may be said against

Antony or against Cleopatra, that either the one or the other is immature in any sense, especially the worldly sense, is a judgment not supported by the play. In so far as love is a symbol of life at its most intense, of the existence of one's self confirmed and illuminated by another self, it exists as an erotic jointure and as a dialogical opposition. Cassirer identifies the most profound contribution of Socrates to our knowledge of the nature of man as the realization that human meaning exists only in dialogical relationship—what Martin Buber, in a warmer phrasing, suggestively calls the I-Thou relationship. When a dialogical relationship is held in plumb by erotic bands, then an ultimate in human experience and human meaning has been achieved. No greater maturity is imaginable than this, the perfect union and perfect equipoise of the lovers of Donne's *Extasie*. Love, in itself, is the mature expression of human nature; if Antony and Cleopatra can be termed immature, then they must be so termed by the standards of Machiavellian policy, of success in the world.

But no one has had more success *in* the world than Antony, and no one has had more experience *of* the world than Cleopatra, and it is precisely this dimension that involves the play so profoundly in final problems— an involvement more complex by far than the one we find in Shakespeare's other play of love, *Romeo and Juliet*. We cannot say that the love of Antony for Cleopatra is deeper than the love of Romeo for Juliet—both loves are absolute expressions of life. In a sense, too, the very oppositeness of the circumstances of the two pairs of lovers makes them equal. Neither pair of lovers is at the very center and fullness of life's experience. Antony and Cleopatra are journeying from it; Romeo and Juliet are journeying toward it, on the entrance step of ecstasy. The jaded, bankrupt tone of the opening of *Antony and Cleopatra* finds its complementing opposite in the expectancy of Romeo and of Juliet. One element in the aging Antony, however, has no counterpart in the youthful Romeo; Antony has had every success in the world, while Romeo has as yet had none. Romeo can give up the world lightly—having nothing, he loses nothing—but Antony is involved as deeply as a man may be involved. He is involved by years, by profession, by achievement. The scope of his character encompasses not only the eternal lover but The Prince. His success and his worldly stature are inescapably apparent in the play. In Philo's opening speech he is the "general," he has a "captain's heart," he is, finally, the "triple pillar of the world." Enobarbus praises him as more dangerous than Octavius: " 'Tis better playing with a lion's whelp," he says, as Antony orders Thyreus whipped, "Than with an old one dying" (III.xiii.94–95). Pompey praises him as the worldly superior of both Octavius and Lepidus: "His soldiership/ Is twice the other twain" (II.i.34–35). He is described in Octavius's opening speech as "our great competitor" (I.iv.3). When confronted by Antony's love, Octavius may find Antony a "boy," but when confronted by Antony's worldly skill and valor, as we see so clearly in his receipt of Antony's challenge to combat, he does not think himself dealing with a boy: "Let the old ruffian know/ I have many other ways to die" (IV.i.4–5). Antony, the "boy" preoccupied by love, becomes the "old ruffian" of worldly affairs. We note with admiration Octavius's honesty with himself: "I have many other ways to die." He does not expect to emerge alive, much less victorious, from an encounter with Antony, and he has the objectivity to admit the fact calmly instead of taking cover behind threats or bombast.

We find it, then, a measure of Octavius's truncated heart and foreshortened experience that he is reduced to describing Antony's love not only as lust but as immaturity, for very shortly afterwards he recalls Antony's worldly prowess in terms of awe:

> Thou didst drink
> The stale of horses and the gilded puddle
> Which beasts would cough at; thy palate then did deign
> The roughest berry on the rudest hedge.

> (I.iv.61–4)

No praise could more explicitly refute the repeated Roman descriptions of Antony as the Epicurean at table and in bed. Antony, in the most trying affairs of the world, has displayed not merely courage in the moment of combat, but a superhuman stamina. And—a final accolade from the Machiavel—Antony has shown the most formidable of worldly virtues: patience—he has shown "patience more/ Than savages could suffer" (I.iv.60–61). In his praise Octavius is not only generous but accurate; the Machiavel cannot afford less than honesty in his analysis of worldly matters. And yet Antony's love for Cleopatra remains nothing more than "lascivious wassails" (I.iv.56). Octavius, the clear-headed rationalist in things of the world, is ineffective—even, to an extent, in worldly terms—because he cannot understand the ways in which the human heart controls the actions of men.

The opening of the second act affords us an opportunity to observe in detail the requirements for success in the world. The scene is Pompey's headquarters at Messina, and we see Pompey as the Machiavel *manqué*. He projects himself grandly into the future, weaving plans and policy in a manner worthy of Octavius:

> I shall do well.
> The people love me, and the sea is mine;
> My powers are crescent, and my auguring hope
> Says it will come to th' full.

> (II.i.8–11)

He reviews for himself the worldly deficiencies of both Antony and Octavius, and concludes by saying:

> Lepidus flatters both,
> Of both is flatter'd; but he neither loves,
> Nor either cares for him.

(II.i.14–16)

Pompey's careless use of the word "love" in describing the people's view of him, and in describing the possibilities of the relationship of Lepidus to the other members of the triumvirate, indicates that for him, as for Octavius, the reality of love does not exist. The indication is strengthened—in a tone once again suggesting Octavius—by his coarse mistaking of Antony's love for lust: "But all the charms of love,/ Salt Cleopatra, soften thy wan'd lip!/ Let witchcraft join with beauty, lust with both!" (II.i.20–22). And he concludes with a reference to "The ne'er lust-wearied Antony" (II.i.38).

To this extent Pompey seems the ideal Machiavel; confidence in the reality of the world, willingness to live in the future, inability to love—all these seem his credentials. But still another element obtrudes in Pompey, a fatal tendency to govern his attitudes by rigid formulas removed from the flux of experience—in this instance the notion of justice. "If the great gods be just," he says in his first utterance, "they shall assist/ The deeds of justest men" (II.i.1–2). The successful Machiavel can scarcely build his policy on the merely hypothetical justice of the merely hypothetical gods. And Pompey allows himself to take seriously the so-called love of the populace. And he thinks of Antony's relation to the world in terms of honor, wishing that "Epicurean cooks" may sharpen Antony's appetite so that "sleep and feeding may prorogue his honour" (II.i.26). Completely involved in the struggle for power, Pompey nonetheless permits himself the luxury of hiding his aims, not from his enemies but from himself. He adopts, with pompous words, the persona of the avenger of his father, of the heir to the idealism of Brutus:

> What was't
> That mov'd pale Cassius to conspire; and what
> Made the all-honour'd, honest Roman, Brutus,
> With the arm'd rest, courtiers of beauteous freedom,
> To drench the Capitol, but that they would
> Have one man but a man? And that is it
> Hath made me rig my navy . . . with which I meant
> To scourge th' ingratitude that despiteful Rome
> Cast on my noble father.

> (II.vi.14–23)

Constricted by dead formulations, his motivations obscured from himself, Pompey cannot survive in the power struggle. "Wilt thou be lord of all the world?" whispers Menas. "What say'st thou?" replies Pompey, fearfully, stupidly, as if his whole stance in life had not been taken in hope and expectation of precisely such an opportunity as has been given him. "Wilt thou be lord of the whole world? That's twice," returns Menas contemptuously. "How should that be?" gasps Pompey, craven and confused. "I am the man/ Will give thee all the world," continues Menas remorselessly. "Hast thou drunk well?" asks Pompey. "No, Pompey, I have kept me from the cup./ Thou art, if thou dar'st be, the earthly Jove" (II.vii.67–73). The sweet fruition of an earthly crown—all that existence can provide for the Machiavel—stands within the grasp of Pompey. "These three world-sharers, these competitors,/ Are in thy vessel," says Menas, "let me cut the cable;/ And, when we are put off, fall to their throats./ All there is thine" (II.vii.76–79). And then Pompey wilts. He flees from the reality he seeks, heaping the sands of his sterile codifications over his frightened head:

> Ah, this thou shouldst have done,
> And not have spoke on't! In me 'tis villany;
> In thee't had been good service. Thou must know,

> 'Tis not my profit that does lead mine honour;
> Mine honour, it. . . .
> . . . Desist, and drink.

(II.vii.79–86)

And with that statement Pompey is destroyed. "For this," mutters Menas, "I'll never follow thy pall'd fortunes more./ Who seeks, and will not take when once 'tis offer'd,/ Shall never find it more" (II.vii.87–90). And so it comes as the expected and unemphasized when we hear later, almost in passing, that Pompey has been murdered by an officer of Antony.

We learn, from the foregoing scene, much about the play's scale of values. We learn of a moral law of excluded middle that dictates that one must cast his lot either completely with the world, or completely with love. The moralistic trimmer has no place. We learn that the abstract formulations—especially as epitomized by honor—do not partake either of the reality of the human spirit or of the reality of the world, but rather are monuments to the absence of reality. When the sea of life recedes, such are the shells left on the shore.

The sterility of honor and the Machiavel's ignorance of love interact elaborately, and both are connected with the Roman view of life. To Octavius honor is merely another agent of policy: he greets Antony, at their meeting in the second act, with the charge of dishonor:

> You have broken
> The article of your oath; which you shall never
> Have tongue to charge me with.

(II.ii.81–83)

Lepidus, terrified by the effect of such words on the proud Antony, interposes frantically: "Soft, Caesar!" But Antony, a Roman now, in a Roman world, replies:

> No,
> Lepidus, let him speak.
> The honour is sacred which he talks on now,
> Supposing that I lack'd it.
>
> (II.ii.84–86)

The sardonic thrust, "Supposing that I lack'd it," suggests a reason for Antony's equanimity. The accusation by Octavius is a worldly gambit, and Antony declines to play it. Honor, in Falstaff's phrase, is "a mere scutcheon"; it really does not exist, except as a cover for Machiavellian policy. Thus Octavius, who so haughtily proclaims that the "article" of his "oath" will never be broken, later instructs Proculeius, with calm mendacity, to go to Cleopatra: "Go and say/ We purpose her no shame" (V.i.61–62). To Dolabella, seconding the embassy of Proculeius, Cleopatra addresses a question, however: "Know you what Caesar means to do with me?" "Though he be honourable,—" replies Dolabella haltingly, and is interrupted by Cleopatra: "He'll lead me, then, in triumph?" "Madam," admits Dolabella, "he will; I know't" (V.ii.106–10). The Machiavellian Octavius stands revealed.

In Roman terms honor is a virtue that functions much like love; that is to say, both honor and love are instruments of policy, neither honor nor love exists on any other level. Octavius, testing still another of his equations for the description of love, offers, with a focusing of both honor and love, his sister Octavia to Antony:

> There's my hand.
> A sister I bequeath you, whom no brother
> Did ever love so dearly. Let her live
> To join our kingdoms and our hearts; and never
> Fly off our loves again!
>
> (II.ii.151–55)

The matter could scarcely be stated more plainly. The marriage of Antony and Octavia will be the instrument "to join our kingdoms and our hearts." So long as kingdoms remain joined, then so long will hearts remain joined, and when kingdoms split, then "loves" fly off. The word "love" in such a context takes on the dissemblance of euphemism. As merely an instrument of policy, such love stands in every possible opposition to the love of Antony and Cleopatra. The world is clearly master. No sooner have Octavia and Antony been wed than Antony explains the basic Roman facts to his bride: "The world and my great office will sometimes/ Divide me from your bosom" (II.iii.1–2). To which Octavia, pliant, assents. When, later, the shortlived alliance of Antony and Octavius begins to split, the "love" of Octavia for Antony and for her brother dutifully attempts to mend the rift:

> A more unhappy lady,
> If this division chance, ne'er stood between,
> Praying for both parts.
> The good gods will mock me presently,
> When I shall pray "O, bless my lord and husband!"
> Undo that prayer by crying out as loud,
> "O, bless my brother!"
>
> (III.iv.12–18)

Confronted by the politic piety of Octavia's kingdom-joining "love," Antony counters falseness with falseness: "Gentle Octavia,/ Let your best love draw to that point which seeks/ Best to preserve it. If I lose mine honour,/ I lose myself" (III.iv.20–23). His "honor" neatly checking Octavia's "love," Antony hies himself back to Cleopatra.

With Cleopatra, however, neither the Roman love nor the Roman honor has currency. In the first act we see Antony, at the ebb tide of his emotion, at the apex of his

Romanness, attempt to employ both as instruments, and Cleopatra rejects them explicitly: "O most false love! . . . Now I see, I see,/ In Fulvia's death, how mine receiv'd shall be" (I.iii.62–65). Pretending illness, she recovers upon Antony's protestation of love, and says:

> I am quickly ill and well,
> So Antony loves.
>
> (I.iii.72–73)

Thus encouraged, Antony attempts to prepare for his departure by the employment of the love-and-honor duality:

> My precious queen, forbear;
> And give true evidence to his love, which stands
> An honourable trial.
>
> (I.iii.73–75)

To which Cleopatra replies, scathingly:

> So Fulvia told me.
> I prithee, turn aside and weep for her;
> Then bid adieu to me, and say the tears
> Belong to Egypt. Good now, play one scene
> Of excellent dissembling; and let it look
> Like perfect honour.
>
> (I.iii.75–80)

She has here unerringly identified the role of honor throughout the play: there is no honor, only the pretense of honor; "perfect honour" is merely a "scene of excellent dissembling." When she sees that he is determined to leave for the meeting with Octavius, she resigns herself to the separation, but does not forbear to add one final spiteful thrust:

> Sir, you and I must part, but that's not it;
> Sir, you and I have lov'd, but there's not it;
> . . . But, sir, forgive me,

> Since my becomings kill me when they do not
> Eye well to you. Your honour calls you hence
>
> (I.iii.87-97)

Cleopatra is impervious to honor, but Octavia is manipulated by its invocation. Pompey manipulates himself by an appeal to honor, but both Antony and Octavius invoke it as an instrument of worldly policy. We note that neither Cleopatra nor Antony nor Octavius appears to regard honor in any other light. Octavius presents himself clothed in honor—"You have broken/ The article of your oath, which you shall never/ Have tongue to charge me with." Antony is not only unruffled by the charge against himself but quite unbelieving of Octavius's own claim to virtue; for when Lepidus—whose position in the triumvirate is guaranteed by the very oath that Octavius claims to uphold—when Lepidus falls, Antony greets the news not, as one might expect of a man devoted to honor as a reality, with a denunciation of Caesar, but rather, revealingly, with a denunciation of Lepidus for having believed Caesar. "Caesar and Lepidus have made wars upon Pompey," says Eros. "This is old," answers Enobarbus, "What is the success?" And Eros replies: "Caesar, having made use of [Lepidus] in the wars 'gainst Pompey, presently denied him rivality . . . and . . . seizes him. So the poor third is up, till death enlarge his confine." "Then, world," says Enobarbus, "thou hast a pair of chaps, no more. . . . Where's Antony?" "He's walking in the garden—thus," replies Eros, "and spurns/ The rush that lies before him; cries 'Fool Lepidus!' " (III.v.5–18). Fool Lepidus, not dishonorable Caesar. Like Pompey, like Enobarbus, Lepidus commits himself fully neither to the world and its Machiavellian laws nor to the counter reality of love, and like Pompey and Enobarbus, Lepidus finds that no place exists between the mighty contenders for the claim to reality. As Octavia comes to learn, there is "no midway/ 'Twixt these extremes at all" (III.iv.19–20). The play rests on bedrock. Negative prescriptions and rigid formulations are inadequate dikes to hold back the tide of the world. We do not need Nietzsche to reveal to us the truth about moral codes: that, while they are ostensibly bulwarks against the world, they become finally instruments of the world. Christ brought a new law. Only love can cope with—and defeat—the world. And love does so not by abstract rule, but by living existence. The world is not blocked by love; the world is rather abandoned by love. Love is not a haven from the world's cruel reality; rather the world is denied reality when love exists.

The play opens. Stagnant in a bankrupt court, Antony and Cleopatra bicker, with only feeble flashes of love to lighten the pall of their world-weariness. For an instant the words "Eternity was in our lips and eyes" make bright the scene. Then the tired distrust settles down again, and Antony departs to make his peace with the morally ascendant world. We see the world, gleaming and devious in the hands of Octavius and Pompey and Lepidus—and Antony, fascinated again by a game he has always played well, plays once more, with elegance and finesse. False vows are smoothly made, treacherous compacts sealed. The world seems to triumph, and to signalize its triumph it dictates the absolute capitulation of love. Octavia and Antony will marry, and by their marriage love will become the servant of the world. The querulous Cleopatra seems far distant. Suddenly the reminiscence of Enobarbus creates her in her moment of splendor: "The barge she sat in . . . a burnish'd throne" (II.ii.196). The great portrait recalls Cleopatra as a presence. "Now Antony must leave her utterly," gloats the lustfully appreciative Maecenas. And then, from the most unexpected source, from the cynical

Roman, the worldly Enobarbus, comes the weight of the Pyramids: "Never; he will not./ Age cannot wither her, nor custom stale/ Her infinite variety" (II.ii.-239–41). And we know then, with the certainty of stone, that the world has met not merely an opponent, but its master.

Antony, meanwhile, married to Octavia, seeks to rationalize his longing for Cleopatra in terms of worldly polity. "The very dice obey him" (II.iii.33), he says of Octavius's worldly successes—not grudgingly, we feel, but almost approvingly. In Roman terms, one does not abandon the world; if one leaves the world, it can only be for reason of defeat. So defeat, then, will Antony accept. And in Roman terms one does not desire a woman for love, but only for lust. So lust, then, will Antony admit: "I' th' East my pleasure lies" (II.iii.40). And later, to Pompey, he describes his love for Cleopatra apologetically: "The beds i' th' East are soft" (II.vi.51). The ignominy of his statement teases us. It is one thing to join in love with the approval of the world and of society, soothed by noble sentiments; it is quite another to be forced back, at the cost of worldly success, with the stigma of social rebuke, to a higher reality. Invulnerable to reproof, the love of Antony and Cleopatra persists. Lust or love, infatuation or dedication—names do not matter. Reality is itself.

So Antony returns to Cleopatra, and her non-existence in his absence is gone. Gone is the boredom, the frustrated sexuality. No more billiards with eunuchs, no more angling for fish, no more shouting at attendants, no more screeching jealousy. Love is; it has no need of alchemy.

And on the other side, the world collects its strength. Octavius marshals the dissembling virtues—reasonableness, objectivity, maturity, restraint—and reviews his case for war: "Contemning Rome," he says of Antony,

> he has done all this and more
> In Alexandria. Here's the manner of't;
> I' th' market-place, on a tribunal silver'd,
> Cleopatra and himself in chairs of gold
> Were publicly enthron'd.
>
> (III.vi.1–5)

He speaks of "the unlawful issue" that Antony and Cleopatra's "lust" has had, and legalistically, he counts:

> His sons he . . . proclaim'd the kings of kings:
> Great Media, Parthia, and Armenia
> He gave to Alexander; to Ptolemy he assign'd
> Syria, Cilicia, and Phoenicia.
>
> (III.vi.13–16)

Antony's complaints he skillfully denigrates:

> Then does he say he lent me
> Some shipping unrestor'd. Lastly, he frets
> That Lepidus of the triumvirate
> Should be depos'd. . . .
>
> (III.vi.26–29)

When Agrippa cautiously says that this last of Antony's
accusations should be answered, Octavius, with off-hand
contempt for truth, says marvelously: "I have told him
Lepidus was grown too cruel" (III.vi.32). Octavius's
character turns to reveal itself in still another aspect
when Octavia, the "sister . . . whom no brother/ Did
ever love so dearly," enters. There is no word of concern
for any possible hurt to Octavia, but only concern for
the forms and trappings of her arrival:

> You come not
> Like Caesar's sister. The wife of Antony
> Should have an army for an usher. . . .
> But you are come

A market-maid to Rome, and have prevented
The ostentation of our love. . . .

(III.vi.42–52)

Having delivered himself of this further attempt to de-
scribe love, Octavius coldly continues: "We should have
met you/ By sea and land, supplying every stage/ With
an augmented greeting" (III.vi.53–55). Octavia pleads
her embassy, and Octavius heartlessly identifies her role
as an "abstract" between Antony and Cleopatra (III.-
vi.61).

In Egypt the moment of decision approaches. Cleopatra matches Antony's sentiment at the opening of
the play—"Let Rome in Tiber melt"—with "Sink Rome,
and their tongues rot/ That speak against us!" (III.vii.-
16–17). Antony, his worldly judgment deserting him in
Cleopatra's proximity, ignores the voices of his worldly
aides, Enobarbus and Canidius, and, faced by the forces
of Octavius, decides to fight by sea—showing once
again that to abandon the world in one thing is to abandon it in all. Octavius arrays his forces. Battle is joined.
Cleopatra leaves the fight—"like a cow in June,/ Hoists
sails, and flies," says Scarus succinctly (III.x.14–15). We
see in her action not merely one last grandly flirtatious
gesture—her "infinite variety"—but also a deliberate
sabotage of Antony's chances for worldly success.
Though Scarus realizes that Antony's side has "kiss'd
away/ Kingdoms and provinces" (III.x.7–8), he mistakenly assumes that "The greater cantle of the world is
lost/ With very ignorance" (III.x.6–7). Unlike Scarus,
Antony explicitly recognizes Cleopatra's deliberate sabotage of the world's claims. "O, whither hast thou led me,
Egypt?" "O my lord, my lord," replies Cleopatra, pretending, "Forgive my fearful sails! I little thought/ You
would have followed" (III.xi.51, 54–56). But Antony,
conscious of his choice, insists upon an equal acknowl-
edgement from Cleopatra: "Egypt, thou knew'st too

well"—and, a second time, "O'er my spirit/ Thy full supremacy thou knew'st"—and, inexorably, a third time, "You did know/ How much you were my conqueror" (III.xi.56, 58–59, 65–66).

Now the fourth and fifth acts of *Antony and Cleopatra* have received profound praise, not only for the unutterable heights to which they carry Shakespeare's diction, but for the technical problems of climax they surmount. With the death of Antony in Act Four the play attains a splendor of language and an expansion of spirit that seem to leave no possibilities of further expression. And this achievement the fifth act must not only sustain, but by virtue of its climactic position in some ways surpass.

It is necessary, by way of prologue to an understanding of these two acts, to place in special focus for ourselves the central position of tragedy; and for this purpose we find the descriptions of Aristotle not wholly adequate. In particular, we may doubt whether the conception of *catharsis,* of a purgation of pity and terror in the onlooker, is not too negative to account for the magnificence and intensity of the emotional process involved in *Antony and Cleopatra*. We may inspect our own emotions and conclude that the presence of joy, not the absence of pity and terror, describes our state at the end of the play. We finish the play not with composure but with exhilaration, and the realm toward which we are directed is not the painless but the beatific.

For tragedy does not deal with death; tragedy deals with life. We see in tragedy not the meeting of an end, but the conduct of an existence. If all of us were immortal in this earthly life, then the bare fact of a man's demise would indeed assume awesome proportions; but we all die, and what matters is not the when of death but the how of life.

The theme of tragedy is life, not death. In the great Shakespearean plays the protagonist always has the choice either of accepting a death that defines his life at its highest level, or of avoiding death and descending to a lower level of life, to a level of breathing non-existence. He is always presented with a choice, and we may thus define the tragic protagonist, in his most basic characteristic, as a being who chooses life rather than death. Nietzsche has counseled us not to look too long into the abyss, for fear the abyss begins to look back into us. For most of us the eye of the abyss early begins to exert an hypnotic power, and our very existences are compromised by its gaze. Man is compounded of being and non-being, and non-being is ever encroaching upon his being. The symbols of the abyss, time and death, ever more powerfully dictate his action. Fear of time causes him to mortgage his present being for the future; fear of death causes him to desert the fullness of life. And in smaller symbols, the abyss, as prudence, as foresight, as all the many trimming virtues of daily life, deludes him with its hypothesis of an existence horizontally extended into unlimited time, rather than an existence vertically elevated into brief eternity. Eternity is the fullness of now, not the unending succession of time—*aeternitas non est temporis sine fine successio, sed nunc stans*. We pawn ourselves for the abyss.

The tragic protagonist allows no such encroachment on his being. He has the choice of affirming his freedom and his being, or of recognizing the dominion of circumstance and the empire of non-being. He chooses to affirm his existence, and in doing so he disregards the abyss, he mocks the midnight bell, and non-being loses its power. We realize that the protagonist acts, and is not acted upon. We realize that love of life, not fear of death, informs his action. The tragic protagonist may be just, or he may be unjust; he may or may not be virtuous; he may or may not be wise; he may or may not have distinction of intellect—the Aristotelian description seems in any case negative and insubstantial. We ask only one thing of the tragic protagonist, that he be truly alive. In Shakespeare's plays it is always the quality of life, as epitomized by the quality of feeling, that identifies the tragic protagonist. The quality of life, not the quality of thought. Hamlet is intellectual; Othello is not. But both feel. The quality of life; not the moral posture. Brutus is just; Macbeth is not. But both feel. And all are truly alive. None of them will be fortune's fool; all of them are always ready to shake the yoke of inauspicious stars. It is the tragic hero's supreme sign of his love of life that he refuses to allow the fear of death to intrude upon life's fullness. We feel no sadness at the death of the tragic protagonist; we feel rather exhilaration at his life. We should speak not of the tragic fall, but of the tragic elevation.

Such an elevation we find in the fourth act of *Antony and Cleopatra*. The issues are joined. Love is being; the world, non-being. We see the world degenerate from its moral ascendancy at the first of the play, and as the world becomes stumbling and uncertain, the at first stumbling and uncertain love of Antony and Cleopatra soars into fire and air. The empire becomes a self-seeking rabble; the whore becomes Cleopatra.

The world's degeneration is emphasized by its abandonment of its proud hallmarks: duty, honor, responsibility, loyalty. "The loyalty well held to fools does make/ Our faith mere folly" (III.xiii.42–43), says Enobarbus, unwilling to take off the cloak of virtue as he prepares to desert Antony and enter the night of non-being—"I will seek/ Some way to leave him" (III.xiii.200–201). The whole empire displays itself as non-being:

> Alexas did revolt and went to Jewry on
> Affairs of Antony; there did persuade
> Great Herod to incline himself to Caesar
> And leave his master Antony; for this pains
> Caesar hath hang'd him. Canidius and the rest

> That fell away have entertainment, but
> No honourable trust.
>
> (IV.vi.12–18)

As the choric support for the world dissolves, Antony becomes more magnificent. Learning of Enobarbus's treachery, he produces from the fullness of his being an action of unworldly generosity:

> Go, Eros, send his treasure after; do it;
> Detain no jot, I charge thee. Write to him
> . . . gentle adieus and greetings;
> Say that I wish he never find more cause
> To change a master.
>
> (IV.v.12–16)

Free at last from the chains of worldly bondage, Antony mounts to a realm of new intensity. We might expect fear on the eve of a battle in which he is foredoomed to defeat. We might expect fear at the prospect of the death that is sure to come. But we find instead a treasuring delight in life—and a sense of life's community for the first time transcends the disruptions bred by power:

> Give me thy hand,
> Thou hast been rightly honest;—so hast thou—
> Thou,—and thou,—and thou. You have serv'd me well,
> And kings have been your fellows.
>
> (IV.ii.10–13)

The last night takes on an aspect of eternity; exhilaration illuminates the darkness:

> Where hast thou been, my heart? . . .
> . . . Come,
> Let's have one other gaudy night. Call to me
> All my sad captains; fill our bowls once more;
> Let's mock the midnight bell.
>
> (III.xiii.172,182–85)

And Cleopatra, re-born, conjoins: "It is my birthday."
In passion and symbolic ambiguity Antony transfigures
the moment: "Wait on me to-night. . . . Tend me to-
night. . . . Tend me to-night two hours . . . burn this
night with torches. Know, my hearts,/ I hope well of
to-morrow. . . ." And the vision of paradise begins to
unfold; death and honor, the attributes of the abyss and
of the world, are prophetically transcended: "I hope well
of to-morrow, and will lead you/ Where rather I'll
expect victorious life/ Than death and honour"
(IV.ii.41–44).

Then, tenderly, Antony, helped by Cleopatra, begins
to armor himself for his climactic encounter with the
world. "Eros! Come; mine armour, Eros!" he commands. "Nay, I'll help too," laughs Cleopatra, "What's
this for?" "Ah, let be, let be! Thou art/ The armourer of
my heart" (IV.iv.2–7), says Antony fondly, and the inconsequence, the childlike carelessness and ease of the
lovers, adds to our growing sense of their freedom.
Everywhere the fearful strivings of a Machiavellian
world begin to transmute themselves into the exhilaration of children at play, secure in their sense of reality:

> That thou couldst see my wars to-day, and knew'st
> The royal occupation! Thou shouldst see
> A workman in't.
>
> (IV.iv.16–18)

Pride of skill well displayed shines through the lines, but
no anxiety. The exhilaration persists, communicated now
to Antony's men: "The morn is fair. Good morrow,
general," says the Captain. " 'Tis well blown, lads," says
Antony happily,

> This morning, like the spirit of a youth
> . . . begins betimes.
> So, so; come, give me that. This way; well said.
>
> (IV.iv.24–28)

So begins the second day of battle. Triumphant, Antony returns to his queen. And we encounter then the lines that constitute the absolute thematic center of the play: Cleopatra greets Antony:

> Lord of lords!
> O infinite virtue, com'st thou smiling from
> The world's great snare uncaught?
>
> (IV.viii.16–18)

It is a perfect moment. In hypostasis stand the pride of Cleopatra, the power of Antony, the exhilaration of the lovers, the discomfiture of the Machiavellian world.

Such a moment cannot be sustained in this life. The world returns to the attack, and Cleopatra once again upsets hopes for worldly victory:

> All is lost!
> This foul Egyptian hath betray'd me.
> . . . Triple-turn'd whore! 'tis thou
> Hast sold me to this novice. . . .
> . . . Betray'd I am.
> . . . The shirt of Nessus is upon me. . . .
> . . . The witch shall die.
>
> (IV.xii.9–10,13–14,24,43,47)

But Antony cannot untie the subtle knot that makes him man. Cleopatra's last love trick, the false report of her death, supplants his Roman rage by the quietness, modulating into a swelling exhilaration, of the soul deciding for eternity: "Unarm, Eros; the long day's task is done,/ And we must sleep. . . ./ . . . since the torch is out,/ Lie down, and stray no farther." (IV.xiv.35–36, 46–47). The renunciation of worldly cares is matched by the recovery of his sense of love: "I will o'ertake thee, Cleopatra, and/ Weep for my pardon. So it must be, for now/ All length is torture" (IV.xiv.44–46). And the language reaches heaven's gate: "Eros!—I come, my queen!—

Eros!—Stay for me!/ Where souls do couch on flowers,
we'll hand in hand . . ." (IV.xiv.50–51). Then the entire
world gives way to love. Honor for the first time partakes
of reality; time is transformed into eternity; Eros the
servant becomes Eros the god. Bare earthly moments
after the report of Cleopatra's death, Antony says:

> Since Cleopatra died
> I have liv'd in such dishonour that the gods
> Detest my baseness. . . .
> Come, then; for with a wound must I be cur'd.
> . . . Come, then; and, Eros,
> Thy master dies thy scholar: to do thus
> I learn'd of thee.
>
> (IV.xiv.55–57,78,101–103)

As Antony dies, Cleopatra makes her own final choice,
to free her world-wearied flesh:

> Shall I abide
> In this dull world, which in thy absence is
> No better than a sty? O, see, my women.
> The crown o' th' earth doth melt. My lord!
> . . . Ah, women, women, look!
> Our lamp is spent, it's out!
>
> (IV.xv.60–63,84–85)

And by her diction Cleopatra reverses the contempt of
all the Epicurean epithets directed toward her love—for
now the world itself becomes, in Horace's phrase, the
"sty of Epicurus."

The final act of the play serves to recast the lovers'
victory in specific terms of Octavius's defeat. The
struggle between Antony and Octavius for power within
the world becomes, in the fourth act, a struggle within
Antony between the world and love, and in this struggle
love emerges victorious. But the attainment of love is
marked not by the defeat of the world but by the

transcending of the world. Antony rises above the Machiavel's categories, and Octavius, the contender for the world, can hardly be presented as a contender for paradise. Antony relinquishes the world to Octavius, and is rewarded by paradise. Love, as total reality, rejects the world. There is no conflict.

In the fifth act the conflict resumes; love defeats the world, and in doing so identifies the world as non-being. The agent of the world's defeat is Cleopatra, and her opponent in the conflict, his stature carefully delineated by the earlier portions of the play, is Octavius.

The fifth act encompasses a Machiavellian battle of deviousness between Cleopatra and Octavius, and Octavius's Machiavellian virtues are immediately recalled, therefore, because of the lapse of his importance in Act Four. Octavius launches into his most emotional speech of the play, a sincere tribute—Agrippa supplies the choric opinion that "Caesar is touch'd"—a sincere tribute to Antony's greatness as a worldling:

> O Antony!
> I have followed thee to this. . . .
> . . . but yet let me lament
> . . . That thou, my brother, my competitor
> . . . my mate in empire,
> Friend and companion in the front of war,
> The arm of mine own body, and the heart
> . . . Hear me, good friends,—
>
> (V.i.35–36,40,42,43–45,48)

At this moment an Egyptian enters with a message, and Octavius's complex, unloving character is revealed; he leaves off in mid-phrase, and says: "But I will tell you at some meeter season./ The business of this man looks out for him" (V.i.49–50). The call of business, of the future, ignominiously overpowers the one feeble call of Octavius's heart. We contrast his coldness toward his fallen companion and antagonist with Antony's own passionate warmth as recalled by Agrippa: "When Antony found Julius Caesar dead,/ He cried almost to roaring; and he wept/ When at Philippi he found Brutus slain" (III.ii.54–56). The immediacy and totality of Antony's emotional involvement, the presentness of his feelings—which we not only hear about from Agrippa, but witness throughout the play—are juxtaposed against the lack of spontaneity in Octavius. When Octavius receives Antony's challenge he orders Maecenas to "laugh at his challenge" (IV.i.6)—orders another man to laugh, we note, but does not laugh himself. Such enslavement of feeling to policy makes Octavius, even in the eyes of his loyal followers, less than Antony. "When such a spacious mirror's set before him," says Maecenas of Octavius's response to the news of Antony's death, "He needs must see himself" (V.i.34–35).

Octavius delegates Proculeius, seconded by Dolabella, to visit Cleopatra and procure her surrender, "Lest, in her greatness, by some mortal stroke/ She do defeat us; for her life in Rome/ Would be eternal in our triumph" (V.i.64–66). He prepares his lies—"She soon shall know . . . How honourable and how kindly we determine for her" (V.i.57–59)—but Cleopatra understands him: " 'Tis paltry to be Caesar;/ Not being Fortune, he's but Fortune's knave,/ A minister of her will" (V.ii.2–4). She, however, will not be Fortune's knave. She reiterates her decision for freedom:

> . . . it is great
> To do that thing that ends all other deeds;
> Which shackles accidents and bolts up change;
> . . . this mortal house I'll ruin,
> Do Caesar what he can.
>
> (V.ii.4–6,51–52)

The contest for the life of Cleopatra begins; Cleopatra struggling for life in death, Caesar for death in life.

Proculeius enters and praises his Machiavel master to Cleopatra. "Be of good cheer./ You're fallen into a princely hand; fear nothing" (V.ii.21–22). We appreciate the irony. Cleopatra surely does not doubt that she is fallen into a princely hand; indeed, the hand of the Machiavellian prince is precisely her main fear—the hand of the Machiavellian prince and the nothingness it signifies. The worldly Proculeius is followed by the worldly Dolabella. "Assuredly you know me," he coaxes. And in evocation of past splendor Cleopatra derides the world of the anti-lovers: "No matter, sir, what I have heard or known./ You laugh when boys or women tell their dreams;/ Is't not your trick?" (V.ii.72–75). Against the encroaching personality of Octavius—fulsomely presented by his sycophants—she summons up the image, stonily huge, of Antony:

> His legs bestrid the ocean; his rear'd arm
> Crested the world. . . .
> For his bounty,
> There was no winter in't. . . . In his livery
> Walk'd crowns and crownets; realms and islands were
> As plates dropp'd from his pocket.
>
> (V.ii.82–83,86–87,90–92)

And she asks Dolabella: "Think you there was or might be such a man/ As this I dream'd of?" (V.ii.93–94). From the abyss of his non-being, the worldly Dolabella confesses his ignorance: "Gentle madam, no." Claims are made for Caesar's honor, claims of no effect upon Cleopatra. Then the two emissaries are supplanted by a third: Octavius himself:

> Take to you no hard thoughts.
> The record of what injuries you did us,
> . . . we shall remember
> As things but done by chance.
>
> (V.ii.117–120)

Smoothness for smoothness, perfidy for perfidy, Octavius and Cleopatra contend. She renders him an account of her possessions, an account which, on the authority of her treasurer, Seleucus, is grossly misstated. "What have I kept back?" says Cleopatra indignantly. "Enough to purchase what you have made known," replies Seleucus (V.ii.147–48). "Say, good Caesar," explains Cleopatra blandly, "That I some lady trifles have reserv'd,/ Immoment toys." We recall Antony's description of her at the opening of the play, "She is cunning past man's thought," and, as she matches Octavius lie for lie, we begin to entertain the possibility that Octavius has met his match on his own ground. Octavius departs, strewing reassurances behind him: "Caesar's no merchant, to make prize with you . . . no, dear Queen; . . . we intend so to dispose you as/ Yourself shall give us counsel" (V.ii.183,185–87). Then Cleopatra, at the conclusion of her passage through the Machiavel's labyrinthine policy, reveals herself cold, clear, and unconfused: "He words me, girls, he words me, that I should not/ Be noble to myself . . . I am again for Cydnus/ To meet Mark Antony" (V.ii.191–92, 228–29). The clown, bearing the deadly asps, makes his entrance, and Cleopatra says:

> He brings me liberty.
> My resolution's plac'd, and I have nothing
> Of woman in me; now from head to foot
> I am marble-constant.
>
> (V.ii.237–40)

Marble-constant, she reveals Octavius's final ignorance of the springs of human life. In his instructions to Thyreus in the third act, Octavius had confidently asserted that "Women are not/ In their best fortunes strong, but want will perjure/ The ne'er-touch'd vestal. Try thy cunning, Thyreus" (III.xii.29–31). We realize that Octavius has underestimated Cleopatra, but that

Cleopatra has not misjudged Octavius. We realize that the Machiavel has met not only his match, but his master.

Earlier, and in fact throughout the play, we have been aware of a centrally ambiguous fact of Cleopatra's character: she is changeable, and she is specifically changeable in love. She herself recalls her earlier attachments when at the end of the first act she warns Charmian against comparing her relationship to Julius Caesar with her love for Antony, for the early days were her "salad days,/ When I was green in judgement, cold in blood,/ To say as I said then!" (I.v.73–75). Against this dismissal of her former attachment we place her pique in Act Two, when, jealous of Octavia, she says: "In praising Antony I have disprais'd Caesar." "Many times, madam," agrees Charmian. "I am paid for't now," says Cleopatra bitterly (II.v.107–108). We note her many-hued past as a factor in Antony's view of her, when, after her first worldly defection, he viciously recalls her earlier liaisons:

> I found you as a morsel cold upon
> Dead Caesar's trencher; nay, you were a fragment
> Of Cneius Pompey's. . . .

> (III.xiii.116–118)

And after her second defection, he is even more brutal: "Triple-turn'd whore! 'tis thou/ Hast sold me to this novice." But now, in Act Five, Cleopatra's infinite variety, which has caused so much worldly woe for Antony, and has raised in our minds the question of her ultimate fidelity—whether the world or love finally commands her loyalties—hardens into a marble constancy that makes her a fit sharer in the eternal life of the colossal Antony. And the infinite variety with which she defeats the world and beguiles Caesar is changed not only into the marble constancy of a woman eager to die for the reality of her love, but undergoes a third, transcending, transformation into spirit itself: "I am fire and air; my other elements/ I give to baser life" (V.ii.292–93). The choric voice exults: "Caesar's beguil'd" (V.ii.326). As she affixes the serpents to her breast, the great words swim past:

> Give me my robe, put on my crown; I have
> Immortal longings in me. Now no more
> The juice of Egypt's grape shall moist this lip.
> ... Methinks I hear
> Antony call; I see him rouse himself
> To praise my noble act; I hear him mock
> The luck of Caesar, which the gods give men
> To excuse their after wrath. Husband, I come!
>
> > (V.ii.283–290)

We realize at last that Cleopatra's infinite variety encompasses not only variety but infinity. The things which are Caesar's are rendered unto Caesar; but Antony and Cleopatra, who love one another, have overcome the world.

Reduction and Renewal
in King Lear

∽ ∽

King Lear, the mightiest of Shakespeare's achieve-
ments, derives much of its strength and size from a
motif of repeated pluralizations. The protagonist in this
play is not a single figure, but a plurality—consists, not
merely of the old king, but of all the figures in the play's
foreground. Thus the theme of discord between father
and child is served by not one, but two, fathers—
Gloucester and Lear. Each father, again, is wracked by
troubles with not one, but a plurality of children. And
this situation, in its turn, ramifies to a plural: Lear's
rejection is pointedly doubled by Goneril and Regan.
Indeed, in this tragedy more than any other we may say
with Dr. Johnson, "Shakespeare has no heroes; his
scenes are occupied only by men." In this tragedy, accordingly, we do not look from inside with, and thereby
favor the special interests of, any one of its participants,
but, in unique remove, we view a universal scene of men
in quest of meaning—of those who are about to die

searching, amid intermixed nothingness, for the form of life.

Such pluralization, and remove, in the protagonistic function is implied by a fundamental unattractiveness in the character of Lear himself—one which prevents us from a full identification of our own prospects with those posited for him. We are all glad to look with Hamlet's eyes; for the affects of Hamlet—youth, intellect, and grace—are attributes we desire for ourselves. But Lear is marked by foolishness, arrogance, madness, and, as a constant in all these variations, by age. Of these defects, it is his age from which we most instinctively recoil. We usually abhor age in ourselves; and in others we think it almost a crime. Age is a disease whose contagion we fear. We feel pity for the old, but also, underneath our pity, an irritation that in its turn masks fright. Age should be put from sight, society seems to feel, and the hiding places are indiscriminately houses, colonies, or cemeteries.

Age is the signal of the approach of death, and we do not willingly contemplate our own deaths. "The end of our race is death," says Montaigne—even as he recognizes that "the remedy of the vulgar is not to think of it." In the daily normality of our lives, death always is characterized, as Heidegger says, by "Unauffälligkeit"—inconspicuousness. Our acceptance of the proposition that "everyone dies" rejects, rather than accepts, our own deaths, for "dieses Man ist Niemand"—this "one" is no one. We can all, from our own experience, credit the existential formula, "Das Man lässt den Mut zur Angst vor dem Tode nicht aufkommen"—we do not allow ourselves to become anxious by thinking too much about death.

Even as we recoil from identifying ourselves with the fortunes of this "poor, infirm, weak, and despis'd old man," however, we realize that his age gains enormous tragic leverage for his action, and that thereby the play is deepened by the very consideration that makes us recoil. "I am a very foolish fond old man," says the king, "Fourscore and upward, not an hour more nor less" (IV.vii.60–1). But as the Bible says, "The days of our years are threescore and ten; and if by reason of strength they be fourscore years, yet is their strength labour and sorrow; for it is soon cut off, and we fly away" (Psalms 90:10). Lear, in short, is a man without a future, a man gazing into the abyss. "O sir, you are old," notes Regan, "Nature in you stands on the very verge/ Of her confine" (II.iv.148–50). Yet that point from which we look forward only to non-being is likewise the vantage point from which we look backward on the fullest reality of existence. Possibility, as Heidegger says, stands even higher than reality; and Lear's age both implies the maximum actualization of life's possibility and involves that final possibility, that refers existence back to itself—the possibility of the non-existence of existence. All our existence is a "being toward death," but in our daily normality we seek to blot out the realization of death and non-being. The character of Lear, however, standing on the precipice of the abyss, forces our attention toward the nothingness that both defines and assaults us. In Lear's action the features of existence are darkened by nothingness, which, in an effect of tragic *chiaroscuro,* paradoxically emphasizes and deepens as it darkens—the actions of Lear, by occurring at the outermost boundary of life, take on added aliveness. Our common sense of such a truth is witnessed by the many variations, in popular literature, on the theme of the man with only a short time to live, and the heightened sense of life that arises from that knowledge.

Thus the character of Lear at one and the same time places the play at the very intersection of the realms of being and nothingness, and diminishes his appeal as a protagonist. To fulfill the need for protagonistic identification we are, accordingly, directed to the perspectives supplied by other characters. The indication of such a pluralizing is one of the functions of the strange introduction to the opening scene, for that action, in formally presenting Edmund to Kent, presents him also to us; and his priority of appearance, together with his youth and vitality, mark him as a possible figure through whose eyes we might see the play. Yet, as Lear's age repels, while his kingship attracts, just so does Edmund's declared bastardy and its attendant villainy temper our willingness to enter the action as partisans of his youth. And as Edmund commands some, but only a limited portion, of the protagonist's perspective, so likewise, from the duplication of his father-child situation with that of Lear, does Gloucester. Moreover, in such a dividing of the function of a main character we are not presented, as in the figures of Antony and Cleopatra, with a merely formal division of what is really a single tragic perspective, but rather with a true fragmentation. Once the viewpoint of the protagonist is fragmented, it becomes impossible to rule out any other strongly active figure from participation.

Thus the action of *King Lear* has no favored perspective for judgment. And this fact points toward one of its deepest motive truths: *King Lear* presents no protagonist because it presents no achieved identity; the movement of the play, in fact, is precisely the quest for identity. "Who am I, sir?" asks Lear of Oswald (I.iv.85). "What dost thou know me for?" asks Oswald of Kent (II.ii.14). "What art thou?" asks Lear of Kent (I.iv.10). "Who is it that can tell me who I am?" shrieks Lear to the winds (I.iv.250). The ironic and changing answers to such questions, both stated and implied, constitute, as meaning and situation dissolve and recombine, the existential unfolding of the play.

If the action of *King Lear* can thus be described, in its largest terms, as a simultaneous search, on the part of all its major characters, for a meaningful self, the arena of search is ironically laid out by the tragedy's time, its place, and its religious reference. From none of these boundary dimensions does there issue help for struggling man, and, joined in their bleakness, they provide mockingly ironic assurance of equal conditions and fair play for all.

The time of the play is before time—its temporal milieu is almost druidical, and its dreamlike earliness is focused by the marvelous pre-mythology of The Fool: "This prophecy Merlin shall make; for I live before his time" (III.ii.95). Likewise the play's landscape, though nominally England, bears none of the comforting insignia of historical England. The bareness of Stonehenge is everywhere, though even the familiarity of Stonehenge itself is absent. The land has no cities, no towns, no villages; neither inn nor church, neither guildhall nor blacksmith's forge, meets our eyes; there are no stores, nor the tradesmen concerned with them, as there are no farms or farmers. Nowhere, in short, do we encounter the daily, and reassuring, activity of a complex society. Dwellings are sparse; trees are sparser still. Seasons are indistinct. *King Lear's* place, like its time, exists in the bleakness of prehistory; castle and hovel, bare heath and bare beach, these are the features of this alien and denuded landscape, situated in a nightmare corner of thought.

But if no comfort exists within this cosmos, none is available from a higher realm either. Both *Hamlet* and *Othello* take place in Christian matrices, and the existence of heaven and hell, good and evil, the morally right and the morally wrong, dictates the final meanings of both plays. Even *Antony and Cleopatra,* though cast in a historical, rather than a theological, mold of references, does not close off the possibility of Christian parallels. But the cosmos of *King Lear* is sealed; the characters, for better or worse, must seek their destinies in the play's arena of space and time. No Christian grace suffuses their lives; no imperatives light their way from on high.

On the contrary, this play addresses its pieties to a specifically pagan theology that is not reducible to Christian coordinates. All the religious obeisances of *King Lear* are ambivalently directed to a significant plurality of "gods." "The gods are just," says Edgar, "and of our pleasant vices,/ Make instruments to plague us" (V.iii.170–1). "O you kind gods," breathes Cordelia (IV.vii.14); "O the blest gods," purrs Regan (II.iv.171); "You ever-gentle gods," invokes Gloucester (IV.vi.221); "The gods reward your kindness," implores Kent (III.vi.6). When the "gods" are specified, moreover, they reveal themselves as part of the mythology of pagan antiquity. Lear refers to "high-judging Jove" (II.iv.231) and swears both by Apollo ("Now, by Apollo" [I.i.161]) and by Jupiter ("By Jupiter, I swear, no" [II.iv.21]; "Away! By Jupiter,/ This shall not be revok'd" [I.i.181–2]).

Yet the pieties attendant upon the play's theology ironically focus the closedness of its tragic cosmos: either the gods do not exist, or they do not care, or they are malign. "Now, gods, stand up for bastards!" shouts Edmund (I.ii.22), as he embarks on the course that will destroy him. "Hear, Nature! hear, dear goddess, hear!" moans Lear (I.iv.297)—and then his situation promptly becomes worse. "Now, gods that we adore, whereof comes this?" asks Albany (I.iv.312)—but the answering voice is only Goneril. "You see me here, you gods, a poor old man,/ As full of grief as age," says Lear (II.iv.275–6)—but either they do not see, or, seeing, do not care, or, caring, delight in his woe; for the roaring storm closes about both the old man and his grief. "By the kind gods," says Gloucester to Regan, " 'tis most ignobly done/ To pluck me by the beard" (III.vii.35–6). But the gods either do not agree with him or do not hear; for the plucking of his beard is followed by the blinding of his sight: "O cruel! O you gods!"—he shrieks (III.vii.70)—and then his other eye is crushed.

In this regard, Gloucester's chilling statement of summary—"As flies to wanton boys, are we to th' gods,/ They kill us for their sport" (IV.i.38–9)—is not only an epigraph for much of the tragedy's action, but an entry into its meaning. The two plurals—"they" with reference to the gods, "us" with reference to mortals— indicate, on the one hand, the ironic godlessness of a cosmos ruled by a plurality of malign or uncaring "gods" rather than God, and on the other, the indefinite, and by the same token, all-inclusive, identity of the object of the play's agonized rite.

In the ascription of malign action to these gods, moreover, the passage echoes an anti-Christian fundamental of ancient Gnosticism, the view—to cite the title of Plotinus's famous tractate against the Gnostics—that affirms "the creator of the cosmos and the cosmos itself to be evil." "World, world, O world!" groans Edgar as his blinded father is led in (IV.i.10–11), ". . . thy strange mutations make us hate thee"). And in such parallels to the Gnostic belief in the evil of the world, and of its creator, we hear not only the opinion of Cerinthus or Marcion, but the muffled reverberation of that yet more dreadful possibility urged by Basilides: that God is nothing.

If the analogies of *King Lear*'s theological matrix with the tenets of Gnosticism emphasize for us the un-Christianity of its religious environment, the ethical implications of such an environment are focused by an-other order of anti-Christian sentiment: Epicureanism. Epicurus believed, or claimed to believe, in the gods; his principle of *prolepsis,* by which all reality is prefigured in the mind, provided him a basis for saying that the gods exist because people think they exist. But for Epicurus the gods had no function in the world; Epi-

curean deity, in the words of Cicero's *De natura deorum,*
was divinity "omnino nihil curantem nihil agentem"—
caring for nothing and doing nothing. Such gods are
scarcely gods at all, and most of antiquity agreed, in
Cicero's words, that "Epicurum . . . verbis reliquisse
deos, re sustulisse"—that Epicurus had retained the
gods in name, but abolished them in fact. The Epicurean
stress on self-pleasure as the aim of existence, accordingly, was always understood to be in fact a
despairing corollary to a bleak conception of a godless
world. "Epicurus," we read in *De natura deorum,* "vero
ex animis hominum extraxit radicitus religionem cum dis
immortalibus et opem et gratiam sustulit"—when Epicurus destroyed benevolent concern and action in the
immortal gods, he tore out religion by the roots from
the minds of men.

Thus the gods in *King Lear,* so unavailingly sum-
moned for witness, justification, and help by its characters, provide, in their Epicurean uncaringness, no
guarantees of moral right or wrong. "Now, by Apollo,
king,/ Thou swear'st thy gods in vain," says Kent (I.i.-
161–2). Where the moral concern of *Hamlet* is a sublime
pondering, in a Christian ambiance, of the question of
good and evil action, the moral concern of *Lear,* in an
apprehension still more sublime, receives its configura-
tions in situations beyond good and evil—makes mankind, alone in an alien world, find its own way to meaning without the signposts of right and wrong. "You
cannot see your way," says the old man to the blinded
Gloucester. "I have no way, and therefore want no
eyes;/ I stumbled when I saw," comes the answer
(IV.i.19–21). Just as there is no protagonist to command
our easy approbation, so likewise does no character fit
into a traditional framework of blame and the ascription
of evil. On the contrary, the rules of moral action in this
world conform more closely to Spinoza's conception of
adequate and inadequate ideas. Such an emotionless, and

at the same time exalted, criterion of success or failure supersedes that ready language by which we identify our own aims as "good" and those of our opponents as "evil." It is one thing to see Goneril and Regan and Edmund as evil; it is another, deeper, more difficult, and finally more human insight to regard them as simply inadequate. Indeed, such rejection of familiar moral coordinates in order to achieve a renewal of existential concern has been repeatedly urged by the deepest words our culture supplies. "I am dead to the law," says Paul, "that I might live unto God" (Galatians 2:19). "All human encounters," insists Reinhold Niebuhr, "must take place within the general presupposition that the difference between 'bad' men and 'good' men, though immediately important, becomes ultimately irrelevant." And in different contexts, and with different aims, thinker after thinker has come to the same realization. "La morale," says Rimbaud, "est la faiblesse de la cervelle"—morality is weakness of the brain. "There is no such thing," says Nietzsche, "as moral phenomena, but only moral interpretation of phenomena." "I am either happy or unhappy, that is all," says Wittgenstein —"It can be said: good or evil do not exist." And from the austere elevation of his unflinching vision, Spinoza tells us that "good and bad, right and wrong" are "mere prejudices," are "mere modes of imagining, and do not indicate the true nature of anything." In the new context of adequacy, we are allowed to "call a thing good or evil, when it is of service or the reverse in preserving our being." Hence the good, to Spinoza, is that "which we certainly know to be a means of approaching more nearly to the type of human nature; by 'bad' we mean that which we certainly know to be a hindrance to us in approaching the type."

In such a radical apprehension, we see Edmund not as evil, but more remorselessly, as inadequate; Goneril and Regan, not as bad, but, in the fullest sense of the term, as unsuccessful. The epithets good and bad have small application to Lear, or to Cordelia, or to Edmund; we may recall the insistence of Socrates that no man would willingly choose anything other than the good—Edmund pants for life as fervently as does Kent, Goneril as sincerely as does Cordelia. In the closed cosmos of *King Lear,* the good is Spinoza's good—the approach to full humanity; and the final judgment of good is a measuring of humanity. The penalty of failure is the forfeiture of humanity; and this deepest truth is signalized in the play by the omnipresence of animal imagery. Since these images were first counted in 1879, critics have repeatedly commented on their pervasiveness—the play incorporates one hundred and thirty-three references to sixty-four different animals—and that pervasiveness establishes the possibility of a universal—and diminished—norm for human dignity. Daughters whose action is inadequate become "Tigers, not daughters" (IV.ii.40). An unjust judge provides an "image of authority" in which "a dog's obey'd in office" (IV.vi.163). A faithless wife becomes a "gilded serpent" (V.iii.84). The problem of the play, in a sense, is to prove that men are not "flies"; to convince us that we should not "think a man a worm" (IV.i.35).

The play's mighty search for human identity therefore imparts to its action a dialectical movement that has no parallels in tragic drama. Where in *Hamlet* we view paradoxical problems without ever impeaching the worth of the moral order—Wittenberg, or fatherhood, or friendship—in *King Lear* all forms of order, all sanctities —the entire structure of things as given—are reduced to an indeterminate flux in order to take shape in new determinations. In *King Lear* every standard of conduct or meaning is progressively overthrown, and the play constructs anew, out of the shards and ruins of human assumptions, the forms in which human meaning consists.

The indispensable motive component of this dialectical movement of the play is that conception utilized in the philosophical analysis of being: nothingness itself. For nothing is the crucible in which being is refined. In this regard we look to that statement in Spinoza's fiftieth epistle that Hegel called the absolute principle of Spinozistic philosophy: "determinatio negatio est"— determination is negation. In order for anything to be, it must not be. If a table is a table, it must not be a chair. If a rose is a rose, it must not be a dandelion. Likewise, in thinking upon the essential, rather than the accidental, being of anything, the mind's abstractions toward that idea are at the same time a *reductio* toward nothingness. If we ask what is the essence of desk, as distinguished from the particular desk before us, we see that its color can be abstracted—for the desk can be gray as well as brown; we see that its material can be abstracted—for it can be metal as well as wood; we see that its number of drawers is inessential, as is its height, its shape, and its other particularities; in short, as we abstract toward essential definition, we move ever closer to negating the desk entirely. Such is the movement of *King Lear*. All determinations of its cosmos are reduced to the brink of nothingness in the search for that which is essential in human life.

Hence, very early in the play, that general formula "ex nihilo nihil fit"—nothing can be made of nothing— which is a derivation from Aristotelian argumentation (e.g., *Physics* I.8), weaves itself into the fabric of the play's language. "What can you say," asks Lear of Cordelia, "to draw/ A third more opulent than your sisters? Speak" (I.i.87–8). And Cordelia's answer tolls the entrance of being's deepest mystery:

> *Cor.* Nothing, my lord.
> *Lear.* Nothing!
> *Cor.* Nothing.

Lear. Nothing will come of nothing. Speak again.

(I.i.89–92)

The repetitions emphasize the spreading effect of the word, and subsequent repetitions ironically broaden its application:

Kent. This is nothing, Fool.

Fool. Then 'tis like the breath of an unfee'd lawyer; you gave me nothing for't. Can you make no use of nothing, nuncle?

Lear. Why, no, boy; nothing can be made out of nothing. (I.iv.141–6)

Whenever the word seeps into situations, ironies multiply. "What paper were you reading?" asks Gloucester of Edmund, as he takes the bait of Edmund's plot against his brother; and Edmund's answer reverberates beyond his intent: "Nothing, my lord" (I.ii.30–31). The word and the conception represent the abyss toward which all the early movement of the play tends; it subsists as the indefinable nadir of identity. "Thou wast a pretty fellow," says The Fool to Lear,

when thou hadst no need to care for her frowning; now thou art an O without a figure. I am better than thou art now; I am a Fool, thou art nothing. (I.iv.210–13)

In this tragedy there is asserted, against Lear's formula that "nothing can be made out of nothing," the deeper truth, in The Fool's words, of a "use of nothing." "The study of being," as Heidegger notes, "comes upon nothing and makes use of it."

Nothing is, however, in its existential function a vortex as well as a limit; hence, its intrusion into *King Lear* involves the play not only in dialectical emphasis, but in dialectical movement as well. "The unity," says Hegel in his *Wissenschaft der Logik,* "whose moments, Being and Nothing, exist as inseparable, is at the same time different from them, and therefore stands to them in the relation of a third: this, in its most characteristic form is Becoming [or] Transition." Thus nothing not only exists in the play, but draws being toward it. Edgar is first posited in a favorable social determination granted him by his father: the good son, the legitimate heir. Under the eroding action of the play's events, his identity dissipates to a less honored determination: "Abhorred villain! Unnatural villain! Unnatural, detested, brutish villain!" (I.ii.81–2). And that identity in turn sweeps lower into the vortex as "the basest and most poorest shape/ That ever penury, in contempt of man,/ Brought near to beast" (II.iii.7–9)—into Tom-a-Bedlam. Yet this *reductio* is revealed as a transition from something toward nothing: "Poor Turlygod! poor Tom!/ That's something yet. Edgar I nothing am" (II.iii.20–31). By the same token, Goneril is reduced, in the language of her father, from "Goneril,/ Our eldest-born" (I.i.54–5) to "Degenerate bastard!" (I.iv.275) and finally to nothing: "Beloved Regan,/ Thy sister's naught" (II.iv.135–6).

But the effect of nothingness in the play is only partly revealed by invocations of its word. Drama demands concrete representations, the clothings of precise designation and metaphorical extension. Undetermined nothing can dramatically indicate a direction of meaning, but not in itself incorporate that meaning. In *King Lear,* accordingly, the reduction toward nothing is represented by varying motifs: that of the dissolution of reason in madness, of the reduction of shelter from castle to hovel, of the deterioration of dress from finery to rags to nakedness itself, of the collapse of identities by disguise or rejection or insanity.

The something prior to nothing that is posited at the beginning of *King Lear* is represented by the pomp and order of Lear's entrance in the first scene. The world we see is a world of ordered hierarchy and of identities guaranteed by such order: a world of "father," "daughter," "husband," "wife," "suitor"; and in a different interlocking, of "king," "duke," "earl," and various subsidiary orders. The meaning of Lear's entrance is prefigured by the brief situation preceding it, for there we meet two "earls," one of whom is a "father," the other a "noble gentleman": "Do you know this noble gentleman, Edmund? *Edm.* No, my lord. *Glou.* My Lord of Kent. Remember him hereafter as my honourable friend. *Edm.* My services to your lordship" (I.i.25–9). Such interplay of courtesy and deference posits and assures the identities of its participants as it immediately precedes the entrance of the king. The grand procession —first a man bearing a coronet, then the king, then the dukes of Albany and Cornwall, next Goneril, Regan, Cordelia—emphasizes in tapestry-like richness the proud and intricate social fabric of this cosmos.

In this first scene, however, there dangles from the tapestry an unwanted thread, which, when grasped, begins to unravel the entire warp and woof of the fabric. For the preliminary to Lear's entrance not only introduces us to the social identity of "earl" and "father," but to a scorned and unwanted identity: "bastard." With the revelation of this fact, the opening encounter becomes bizarre; instead of that affirmation of social order and continuity we might expect in a father's introduction of his son to a friend, we find, at the very outset of the play, a man rejected by a figure who has "so often blush'd to acknowledge" his son that now he is "braz'd to't," a father who, in jovial bravado, identifies his progeny as a "knave," as a "whoreson" (I.i.10–24). And thus the scene, as it introduces us to a man without a place—an "illegitimate" man—also introduces us to the callousness that, expanding into the attitudes of Lear toward his daughters and subordinates, wedges the first cracks in the play's initial order of assurances.

In the opening encounter we view two men, in coördinates of security and identity, and a third, in coördinates of rejection, disorientation, and abandonment. For Edmund is the abandoned man, the outsider. The very twoness of Kent and Gloucester as earls serves to highlight Edmund's aloneness. In the character of Edmund we see the outcast, the man without proper reference to the expectations of life, without proper antecedents, without proper bulwarks of affection, without acceptable goals. His origin is obscure and tainted, his future without form.

But Edmund the outcast uncovers in the play, by that fact, the universal "Unheimlichkeit"—a forlorn and uneasy sense of psychic homelessness—that Heidegger analyzes as a primordial fact only temporarily assuaged, for all of us, by the securities and assurances of life. Edmund the outsider is marked by an overwhelming sense of "Geworfenheit"—thrownness; he came "to the world before he was sent for" (I.i.22). As Lear, despite the permanence and security implied in his state as king and father, introduces by his age the existential realization of universal "Verfallen"—that is, dissipation and passing away—so in the play does Edmund orient attention to man's true condition of estrangement and alienation. The outsider, the thrown man, is revealed as standing at the very center of the play's axes of assurance. Into the vertical relationships by which society subsists—father bequeathing to son—interposes the bastard, the illegitimate man. Into the horizontal order by which society exists—peer saluting peer—interposes the bastard, the illegitimate man.

Juxtaposed in his singularity against the placings of society, interposed in his illegitimacy at the center of that society, Edmund, the bastard, opens a doorway to nothingness. Ironically, the realm of the legitimate almost immediately begins to dissipate; Edmund, the alone, is joined by another outcast: Cordelia, the beloved. "Here I disclaim," says Lear in his arrogance,

"Propinquity and property of blood,/ And as a stranger to my heart and me/ Hold thee from this for ever" (I.i.115–18). And the pluralization continues: Kent joins Edmund and Cordelia in psychological abandonment and social alienation. "Hear me, recreant!" thunders Lear from his blind belief in his own security, ". . . turn thy hated back/ Upon our kingdom" (I.i.169–79). The new society of outcasts continues to grow. "Legitimate Edgar" joins Kent, the former favored courtier, and Cordelia, the former favored daughter, in estrangement and rejection. "Let him fly far," roars the once fond father, Gloucester, "Not in this land shall he remain uncaught;/ And found,—dispatch" (II.i.58–60). And finally Lear and Gloucester, those who reject, are themselves rejected and cast out into the night of "Geworfenheit": "In such a night/ To shut me out! . . . In such a night as this!" agonizes Lear (III.iv.17–19); while, already deep in the night of blindness, Gloucester in turn is cast out: "Go thrust him out at gates," hisses Regan (III.vii.93).

But that postern door in the castle of society, which so readily opens outward to admit new members to Edmund's desolate company, is not double-hinged; Edmund cannot go in. And all the goals of his action are ironically nullified by this fact. His acceptance of the identity of bastard, and his willingness to act the role of villain, are partly the result of his belief in his freedom: place and identity are only temporary; man is not a link in a chain of necessity, but a totally free agent, and can therefore change his situation. Such an insistence, especially as marked in the play by Edmund's contempt for his father's belief in astrological signs and the portents of things to come, provides close analogy to the Epicurean attitude toward man's predicament. "Nihil tam inridet Epicurus," says one of Cicero's interlocutors, "quam praedictionem rerum futurarum"—nothing stirs Epicurus to ridicule so much as the prediction of things to come. Indeed, three emphases supplied by Edmund's dialogue with his father in the second scene of the first act find explicit parallel in the Epicurean vaunts of *De natura deorum*. Gloucester says that

> These late eclipses in the sun and moon portend no good to us . . . nature finds itself scourg'd by the sequent effects
> (I.ii.112–15)

Edmund then comments that

> This is the excellent foppery of the world, that, when we are sick in fortune,—often the surfeits of our own behaviour,—we make guilty of our disasters the sun, the moon, and stars. . . . An admirable evasion of whoremaster man, to lay his goatish disposition on the charge of a star!
> (I.ii.128–39)

And such contempt for astrological necessity and divination is a concomitant to an amoralism in which Edmund expects to grow and prosper:

> Thou, Nature, art my goddess; to thy law
> My services are bound.
> . . . I grow; I prosper.
>
> (I.ii.1–2,21)

Attitudes of this kind are adumbrated in the dialogical situation of Cicero's treatise, where Velleius the Epicurean attacks the Stoic belief in a destiny controlled by an "unbroken sequence of causation":

> What value can be assigned to a philosophy that thinks that everything happens by fate? . . . if we consented to listen to you . . . we should be devotees of soothsayers, augurs, oracle-mongers, seers and interpreters of dreams. But Epicurus has set us free from superstitious terrors and delivered us out of captivity, so that we have no fear of beings who, we know, create no trouble for themselves and seek to cause none to others, while

we worship with pious reverence the transcendent majesty of nature.

But Edmund—"his terroribus ab Epicuri soluti et in libertatem vindicati"—Edmund the unsuperstitious, Edmund the free, Edmund the maker of his own destiny, is more shackled in human bondage than any other figure in the play. Even as he laughs at the thought that we are "villains on necessity, fools by heavenly compulsion, knaves, thieves, and treachers by spherical predominance" (I.ii.132–4), he foresees a future wholly determined by a word and a phantom conception: "bastard." All his hopes and plans are hypothecated to the transformation of illegitimacy to possession, and his future is projected as one of strict compulsion—as we realize from the obsessive repetitions of the thought of bastardy and legitimacy:

> Wherefore should I
> Stand in the plague of custom, and permit
> The curiosity of nations to deprive me,
> For that I am some twelve or fourteen moonshines
> Lag of a brother? Why bastard? Wherefore base?
> When my dimensions are as well compact,
> My mind as generous, and my shape as true,
> As honest madam's issue? Why brand they us
> With base? with baseness? bastardy? base, base?
> ... Legitimate Edgar, I must have your land,
> ... Fine word "legitimate!"
> Well, my legitimate, if this letter speed
> And my invention thrive, Edmund the base
> Shall top th' legitimate.
>
> (I.ii.2–21)

Preening himself on his freedom, Edmund thus becomes what he scorns, a villain by necessity, a fool and knave by compulsion.

Nor does the frantic course of action upon which he

triumphantly embarks succeed in uncovering the one order of concern that might free him from his bondage. Edmund tells Edgar to "draw, seem to defend yourself," and, after Edgar has completed the charade and departed, Edmund stabs himself in his arm—"Some blood drawn on me would beget opinion/ Of my more fierce endeavour" (II.i.35–6). Gloucester enters. "Now, Edmund, where's the villain?" he asks with threatening fatuity (II.i.39). "Here stood he in the dark . . ." replies Edmund. "But where is he?" presses Gloucester. And then Edmund, from the cover of his stratagem, compresses into one exclamation the depth of his love-starvation: "Look, sir, I bleed." And he has bled, since his very birth—the anguish of a lifetime of neglect pleads for attention. But Gloucester, the man who cannot see until his eyes are gone, looks through and past his bleeding son toward nothing. "Look, sir, I bleed" is answered only by the reiteration of monstrous self-absorption: "Where is the villain, Edmund?" (II.i.40–43).

In Gloucester's word "villain" we hear the echo of one of *King Lear*'s most mocking substitutions of nothing for something. The term appears most frequently in the first three acts of the tragedy, where it reveals itself as an ironical component in the degeneration of society's hierarchical definition of identities. And since in ordinary speech the word "villain" possesses an exorcistic overtone, accordingly, when the first cracks and discords appear in the social assurances of the play, the characters, with humankind's universal readiness to ascribe outer blame rather than reform the inner heart, at first repeatedly attempt to identify a "villain" as the cause of their woes. In the context of a bleakly unassuring cosmos, however, such attempts at easy moral categorization assume the ludicrous inconsequence of a blindfold game. "Unnatural, detested, brutish villain!" rages Gloucester to Edmund, "Go, sirrah, seek him; I'll apprehend him. Abominable villain! Where is he?" (I.ii.80–84). The question is rich in irony: where, indeed, is the villain? "I do not well know, my lord," answers Edmund (I.ii.85). Though Gloucester confidently identifies Edgar as the "villain," Edgar himself, in innocent disclaimer of the identity, points elsewhere: "Some villain hath done me wrong," he confides to Edmund (I.ii.180). And Regan identifies the "treacherous villain" as Gloucester himself (III.vii.87). "Turn out that eyeless villain," echoes Cornwall in certain confirmation of his wife's insight (III.vii.96).

The effect of such wholesale blame is to diminish the importance of blame. It is not that the characters are always inaccurate in their identification of a wrongdoer, or that they are mistaken in their sense of themselves having been wronged. On the contrary, almost everyone wrongs everyone else. "Did my father strike my gentleman for chiding of his Fool?" asks Goneril (I.iii.1), and when Oswald answers in the affirmative, her subsequent remark seems justified: "By day and night he wrongs me" (I.iii.3). But the question, "Did my father strike my gentleman for chiding of his Fool?" suggests, in its lilting tit-for-tat, a childish merry-go-round of blame's cause and effect. The problem of the play's characters is not the fixing of just blame, but how to achieve fullness and meaning in life. Indeed, it is irrelevant whether, as Goneril says to Lear, "You strike my people; and your . . . rabble/ Make servants of their betters" (I.iv.277–8), or whether, as Lear says to Goneril, she is really "a thankless child" (I.iv.311). Goneril is clearly justified in saying "He always lov'd our sister most" (I.i.243)—but the remorseless law of life is that action predicated on self-pity does not lead to recompense. Likewise, part of Lear's purgation is to realize the irrelevance of his claim that "I am a man/ More sinn'd against than sinning" (III.ii.59–60). We, as spectators, weep for the heartbreak of his rejection by his daughters; but he, as participant, can do so only at the cost of deeper descent into non-being: "O Regan, Goneril!" he laments in self-pity, "Your old kind father, whose frank heart gave all,"—but then he catches himself and says, "O, that way madness lies; let me shun that;/ No more of that" (III.iv.19–22). The recrimination of Lear's "I gave you all" (II.iv.253) can always be countered by the recrimination of Regan's "And in good time you gave it" (II.iv.253). Self-pity and recrimination, in this tragedy as in our own experience, only lead deeper into sorrow; the way to light takes another direction. It is not until the imputation of wrong-doing by others is abandoned that the fogs begin to lift: "I did her wrong—" muses Lear suddenly at the end of the first act, and such words, the first of their kind, glimmer as the dawn of a new horizon of life (I.v.25).

The search for the villain, therefore, is an index to the true moral fault in the world of *King Lear:* an inturning self-preoccupation from which, at the outset of the play, none of the characters is entirely free. Goneril and Regan, it is true, are poisonous with malice; Edmund, seething with envy and resentment. But lack of affection breeds such ugliness; and the fact that Cordelia, Edgar, and Kent are more confident, more easy, and more attractive than those who have been rejected is not surprising in view of their flattered and favored positions. Cordelia is indeed sweet—but she is also stubborn with self-esteem. And Edgar, by his complacent and longstanding acceptance of Edmund's unequal share of security and affection, seems less faultless on second glance than he does at first. Even Kent's virtue of plainspoken honesty is one for which he has heretofore been rewarded rather than deprived; and in this respect Cornwall's sarcastic gibe is not wholly without point: "This is some fellow/ Who, having been prais'd for bluntness, doth affect/ A saucy roughness" (II.ii.101–3).

But the norm of self-preoccupation and its corollary,

the callous disregard of others, finds its most arrogant
representation in the actions of the fathers at the beginning of the play. Both Gloucester and Lear insist on the
morality by which children honor their parents ("The
offices of nature, bond of childhood,/ Effects of courtesy,
dues of gratitude" [II.iv.181–2]), and for this very reason their ignorance of their counter responsibilities is the
more grotesque. The alacrity with which both fathers
abandon humanly irrevocable commitments brands them
as blind, arrogant, and callous men: "I never got him,"
says Gloucester in repudiating Edgar (II.i.80); "I disclaim all my paternal care," says Lear in repudiating
Cordelia (I.i.115). Yet such statements are implied from
the outset, on the one hand in the attitude that can make
sport of an illegitimate son, and on the other in the
attitude that can speak of divisions into three, and then
in simpering and logic-bending favoritism conceive "A
third more opulent than your sisters" for Cordelia
(I.i.88). But the absolute measure of the stupidity to
which total self-absorption reduces itself is Lear's unthinkable statement to Cordelia: "Better thou/ Hadst
not been born than not t' have pleas'd me better"
(I.ii.236–7).

Such a statement indicates the true coördinates—inadequate understanding and callous selfishness—that
frame the pomp, and the pretence to meaning, of the
opening of *King Lear*. Accordingly, as has often been
pointed out, the task of the play may be seen, in rich
paradox, as the education of Lear. We associate age
with wisdom, and think of education as a process re-
served for youth (and the Greek *paideia*—education—
incorporates the bias into its very etymology). But Lear,
though he knows nothing except himself, paradoxically
knows not even that: he has, as Regan notes, "ever but
slenderly known himself" (I.i.297). "Thou shouldst not,"
The Fool says with rending truth, "have been old till
thou hadst been wise" (I.v.48). "As you are old and

reverend," says Goneril, you "should be wise" (I.iv.261).
And the theme of Lear's second childhood—that is, a
time of madness and also a time of education—is
grotesquely echoed in various statements of the play.
"Now, by my life," says Goneril, "Old fools are babes
again" (I.iii.18–19). When Lear departs raging into the
night, Goneril speaks with the tone of one supervising a
child's education by harsh experience: " 'Tis his own
blame; hath put himself from rest,/ And must needs
taste his folly" (II.iv.293–4). "To wilful men," agrees
Regan, "The injuries that they themselves procure/
Must be their schoolmasters" (II.iv.305–7).

But Lear's education is only the most paradoxical
instance of a process of learning imposed, as the very
condition of life, on all the characters of the play. The
mode of instruction is not the transmitted truisms of a
schoolroom, nor is its end knowledge. The mode is
rather the radical humiliation prescribed by Montaigne
as the only antidote to man's presumption. "The conviction of wisdom is the plague of man," we read in the
Apologie de Raimond Sebond—"It would seem that
nature, to console us in our wretched and forlorn state,
has allotted to us only presumption." The aim of his
corrosive work, says Montaigne, is "to crush and tread
under foot human pride and arrogance, to make men
sensible of the inanity, the vanity and insignificance of
man"—and, in explicit congruence to the process of
King Lear—"to wrest out of their fists the miserable
weapons of reason." The pride, arrogance, and presumption to wisdom of the men in *King Lear*'s world are, in
their reductions toward nothing, purged by just such an
education; and the greatest reduction of all, the change
in society's norm from reason to madness, follows the
prescription of Montaigne and thereby reveals itself not
merely as the most awesome of all dramatic expositions
of derangement, but at the same time as the one most
integral to the furtherance of a plot. "Wherein consists

the most subtle madness but in the most subtle wisdom?" asks Montaigne; *Lear* accepts the implication of such a question, and ironically reverses its terms—for in this play the discourse of madness alone leads to wisdom.

Indeed, the educational process in *King Lear* not only traverses the pathway from inadequate something to essential being, but admits of no passage alternate to the way of humiliation in the stormy night of nothingness. Though side by side with the motif of ejection into that night is a motif of attempt to withdraw from the storm of life, both motifs are metaphors for futile endeavor. "Alack, the night comes on," says Gloucester (II.iv.303) —but the night comes on for everyone, not only those who are forced into it, but those who retreat from its storms. "Let us withdraw; 'twill be a storm," says Cornwall (II.iv.290), and his words serve as motto for all those characters—Goneril, Regan, Edmund, Cornwall— who are unable to progress beyond their inadequacy. "Shut up your doors," says Regan in confident belief that she has found the way to cope with the night and storm; and Cornwall joins in her belief: "Shut up your doors, my lord; 'tis a wild night:/ My Regan counsels well. Come out o' th' storm" (II.iv.307, 311–12).

But those who retreat from night and storm retreat also from our concern; and it is one of the remarkable feats of Shakespeare's dramaturgy that while his madmen become ever more pertinent and prophetic, the plots, plans, and strivings of those who "come out o' th' storm" congeal, as the play progresses, to an unmemorable indication of indistinct action. Their convulsive efforts only bog them deeper in frustration and defeating paradox. "To both these sisters have I sworn my love," says Edmund (V.i.55), but his boast, by its very pluralization, reveals its emptiness of the meaning of love; and the sisters themselves, so close to one another in adversity, become in their seeming prosperity "Each jealous of the other as the stung/ Are of the adder"

(V.i.56–7). Their castles seem prisons rather than shelters, for what they really need is to open their "self-cover'd" lives (IV.ii.62). In contradistinction to the restorative medicine with which Cordelia's doctor revives Lear, the "medicine" of Goneril paradoxically leads to death: "Lady, I am not well," says Regan in one of the simply stated but endlessly reverberating utterances that fill this play—"Sick, O, sick!"; and Goneril's whispered rejoinder is "If not, I'll ne'er trust medicine" (V.iii.73, 95–6). We find that Edgar's cry, "King Lear hath lost" (V.ii.6), refers only to the pointless struggle for power—the true losers are Goneril, Regan, and Edmund, who forfeit their humanity and prey on one another "Like monsters of the deep" (IV.ii.50). By the end of the play they no longer command concern, and their deaths are as bitterly without importance to others as their lives have been without meaning to themselves. "Your eldest daughters have fordone themselves,/ And desperately are dead," says Kent; but their spiritual death occurred long before, as Lear emphasizes by his abstracted reply, "Ay, so I think" (V.iii.290–91). Immediately afterward, a messenger announces, "Edmund is dead, my lord," to which Albany replies: "That's but a trifle here—" (V.iii.294–5).

Those, on the contrary, who suffer the reduction of their identities and their world are rewarded, not necessarily by happiness, but by intensified existence. The reductive process is accompanied not only by the abolition of selfish identities in a hierarchical order, but by a palpable deepening that contrasts to a shallow unreality obtaining at the play's outset. For the pomp and ceremony of the opening scene are not only colored like a tapestry, but dimensioned like one as well. The shallowness, and the remoteness from existential concern, of the opening action are attested by the simple fact of Lear's division of his kingdom; for in the pieties of Elizabethan statecraft such division was both a mark of incompetence and a herald of disaster. "O king," says the choric counselor in *Gorboduc:*

> To part your realm unto my lords, your sons,
> I think not good for you, ne yet for them,
> But worst of all for this our native land.
> Within one land one single rule is best:
> Divided reigns do make divided hearts.

But in addition to the formulaic depthlessness implied by Lear's act, a two-dimensional, fairy-tale overtone pervades the language of the division: "Know that we have divided/ In three our kingdom," intones Lear (I.i.38–9), and the juxtaposition of king, number, and simple statement engages familiar motifs of the nursery: a king calling for his fiddlers three, or a king in his counting house with numbered blackbirds in a pie. Indeed, the fairy-tale overtone of action and statement reinforces the play's legendary, dreamlike placement in space and time, and hauntingly occurs in various later contexts. When Cornwall commands that Kent be put in the stocks, his comment picks up the vivid but trivial particularities of the child's story: "As I have life and honour,/ There shall he sit till noon" (II.ii.140–1). When Lear madly arraigns Goneril, his specification of charges lilts with the cadence and content of the nursery rhyme: "I here take my oath before this honourable assembly, she kick'd the poor king her father" (III.vi.48–50). And Lear's daughters themselves call to mind, at the outset, the grouping of the two wicked sisters against the good youngest sister that so frequently occurs in children's literature.

But Lear's demand for an accounting of these daughter's love as a condition to dividing the kingdom does not merely follow the pattern set by a fairy-tale conception of a ruler's arbitrariness; it also activates, in lengthy irony, a reductive process. In asking for an accounting of love—the qualitative intensity of the most mysteriously human relationship—Lear relies on the two-dimensional, and wholly irrelevant, conception of quantity: so much love equals so much land. Remorselessly, and ironically, the play turns quantity against him. His hundred knights, the adjunct of his identity and arrogance, are systematically reduced. Goneril—in fairy-tale simplicity—insists that he halve the number. The king, in thunderous reaction, cries, "I can stay with Regan,/ I and my hundred knights" (II.iv.233–4)—but promptly Regan suggests still further reduction: "bring but five and twenty; to no more/ Will I give place or notice" (II.iv.250–2). And the reductive process, in diminishing Lear's retinue, not only begins paring his hierarchical identity, but pointedly re-engages his initial folly by which the qualitative meaning of love is dissipated in quantity. To Goneril he says, "Thy fifty yet doth double five and twenty,/ And thou art twice her love" (II.iv. 262–3). Yet the reduction continues: "What need you," replies Goneril, "five and twenty, ten, or five" (II.iv. 264). And the point is relentlessly driven toward the quantitative symbol of nothing: toward zero. "What need one?" asks Regan finally (II.iv.266).

The reduction of Lear's knights simultaneously spins him toward an understanding of his true self and vibrates with the poignant hurt that in this play reflects human mystery: a hurt that Shakespeare's language can indicate even when no basis of sympathy seems to exist in the situation. Yet, his pain at their diminution notwithstanding, the knights clearly function as an index of Lear's arrogance and self-absorption. The knights, indeed, are useless to Lear; they move, as Goneril indicates, only in that world which holds Edmund in its iron bondage: "Epicurism and lust" (I.iv.265).

The reduction of the knights is only one aspect of the descent toward nothing. Not only does the movement from castle to hovel, from fair weather to storm, signalize, in terms of landscape, the pervasiveness of the world's disintegration, but special reductions permute in differing degrees of irony. In some instances the motif of pluralization additionally extends the depth of the reductive movement. Thus both Kent and Edgar diminish not merely from socially-guaranteed identity to the state of an outcast, but they then proceed to still lower forms. Kent, the earl, after he has "raz'd my likeness" (I.iv.4), becomes Kent the loyal servant. But then he slips lower, to the identity of the-man-in-the-stocks. Edgar, the legitimate son, descends first to Edgar the villain, and then slips lower, to Tom-Turlygod. And Goneril's position in the language of the play is reduced from inheriting daughter to "Degenerate bastard," and from that low rung of humanity to the state of animal: "Detested kite" (I.iv.284). And then, in a wonderful effect of madness's dislocated semantics, she slips even lower in the scale of being. As the fools and madmen arraign the women who are not there, the gathered ironies enclose Goneril's identity. "Come hither, mistress. Is your name Goneril?" says The Fool to her imaginary presence. "She cannot deny it," interposes Lear triumphantly. But Lear's mad gaze has fastened on an object not seen by The Fool— "Cry you mercy," apologizes The Fool to Goneril-imaginary, "I took you for a joint-stool" (III.vi.51–5).

The joining of pluralization to reduction achieves a convulsively shuddering effect of woe in one of the play's most dismal situations. "Who is't can say," muses Edgar, " 'I am at the worst'?/ I am worse than e'er I was" (IV.i.27–8)—and this sense of ever-deeper immersion in the pool of nothingness permeates the action of Gloucester's blinding. "Upon these eyes of thine I'll set my foot," says Cornwall (III.vii.68). But his act, delayed and divided, becomes a plural event. Cornwall's boot descends, but then Regan's terrible remark calls for a symmetry of the unspeakable: "One side will mock another; th' other too" (III.vii.71). It is several lines later, after intervening action, that the second event occurs. "My lord, you have one eye left," calls the dying servant, but his remarks herald a repetition of terror: "Lest it see more, prevent it. Out vile jelly!/ Where is thy lustre now?" (III.vii.83–4).

Gloucester's blinding is a violent extreme for the motif of reduction. The contrasting nadir of Lear's descent is less dramatically horrifying, but, by bringing many meanings to focus, more absolute. From early in the play reductions in identity, as they are revealed on the stage, have implied a corresponding deterioration in costume. A servant is more poorly dressed than an earl; a Tom-a-Bedlam is a mere patchwork of rags. As the security of the castle is increasingly abandoned, and as the threat of the alien storm howls into more dominating presence, an ironic fillip is accordingly added to the reduction movement by diminishing still more the small protection of clothes against the elements. The relation of a house to a dweller is a common trope for the relation of body to soul—as, for instance, the "fading mansion" of the "poor soul" in Shakespeare's own sonnet 146. But equally common—and thereby linking castlehovel reductions to clothes diminutions—is the projection of the relationship as a clothes-to-body trope. Thus one of the statements in Marvell's *The Garden* has "My Soul" casting "the Bodies Vest aside"; and such images are part of the Platonist heritage from antiquity—as, for instance, in Porphyry, *De antro nympharum* 14: "the body is a garment with which the soul is invested." Hence Lear, in confronting both physically and psychologically the full fury of the elements, implies also the philosophical uncovering of the essential being of man:

> Thou wert better in a grave than to answer with thy uncover'd body this extremity of the skies. Is man no more than this? Consider him well. Thou ow'st the worm no silk, the beast no hide, the sheep no wool, the cat no perfume. Ha! here's three on's are sophisticated! Thou art the thing itself; unaccommodated man is no

more but such a poor, bare, forked animal as thou art.
Off, off, you lendings! come, unbutton here.

(III.iv.105–14)

And then he tears off his clothes to reveal the reduction
of the King of the Hundred Knights to a poor, bare,
forked animal. The passage plumbs the abyss. And its
reverberations are increased by parallel emphases in the
Apologie de Raimond Sebond—one of the tiny handful
of works not wholly beggared by comparison with
Shakespeare's masterpiece. "In truth," says the sardonic
Montaigne,

> when I imagine man quite naked . . . I find that we
> have more reason than any other animal to cover our-
> selves. We are to be excused for having borrowed from
> those that have been more favored by nature than our-
> selves, for having decked ourselves with their beauty,
> and concealed ourselves under their spoils of wool,
> feathers, hair, and silk.

And the appropriateness of clothes reduction as a means
of indicating the most total exposure of man, not only
physically, but psychically, to alien elements is obliquely
witnessed in Heidegger's formulation, "Die Angst äng-
stet sich um das nackte Dasein als in die Unheimlichkeit
geworfenes"—the source of foreboding is the thought of
naked existence cast out into "Unheimlichkeit"—into
psychic homelessness.

Lear leads the descent of an entire society to the blank
bottom of "Unheimlichkeit." The Fool alone has always
dwelt there. And as the characters hurled from the doors
of the castle arc downward toward nothingness, their
trajectories are intersected, just as they enter the realm
of madness and night, by the lowly movement of this
"pretty knave." For The Fool—of whose origins and
previous literary variations we may read in Enid Wels-
ford—attains new meanings in the perspective of *Lear*'s

tragic action. Even Edmund, the outcast bastard, has
the attribute of reason; but The Fool stands lower yet
than this irreducible measure of humanity's place in the
cosmos. In terms of the hierarchy obtaining at the first
of the play, The Fool is both free from classification (as
the companion of the king, he alone is licensed to speak
as an equal to even the highest identities of the hierarchy—"your all-licens'd Fool" is Goneril's descriptive
epithet [I.iv.220]), and at the same time is placed at the
absolute bottom of its recognitions. "I am better than
thou art now," he says to the king, "I am a Fool, thou
art nothing" (I.iv.213–14)—but in the very statement
we realize that, in the social hierarchy of the world, all
identities are more honored than that of The Fool, and
that nothing, and only nothing, occupies the space below him.

By the ambivalence of the conception that both places
him below society and frees him from society, The Fool
exerts enormous ironic pressure on the theme of hierarchical place and identity. Unlike Edmund, whose ef-
fort is to crawl to a higher rung in the hierarchy, The
Fool, despite his lowly station, moves in a tranquil and
mysterious plane not subject to the reductions and fall-
ings off of the other characters. "I had rather be any
kind o' thing than a Fool," he begins wistfully—"and
yet I would not be thee, nuncle" (I.iv.202–4). When
Kent salutes his resonating utterance with the recognition that "This is not altogether fool, my lord," The
Fool's telling retort indicates his curious tranquility in
his own being:

> No, faith, lords and great men will not let me; if I had
> a monopoly out, they would have part on't. And ladies,
> too, they will not let me have all the fool to myself;
> they'll be snatching.   (I.iv.165–9)

The Fool first enters the play as the rejected characters
approach the domain of nothingness, remains only long

enough to kindle the spark of human concern in Lear's heart, and then departs. His utterance, rich with inter-folded irony, both serves as the choric norm of the new society of madness and points the way to the mysterious transcendence that lifts the play above nothingness.

Though The Fool lacks the reasoning power that mankind holds aloft to distinguish itself from the beasts, that lack is not, in the school of Montaigne, a matter of deep concern. "We have indeed," says Montaigne, "strangely overestimated this precious reason we so much glory in, this faculty of knowing and judging." On the contrary, The Fool possesses the secret of a more precious attribute than knowledge: the secret of humility. In a world of hatred, divisiveness, and the competition for power and affection, a world of self-absorption, arrogance, and ignorance, The Fool moves serenely, complaining little, blaming less. And his simplicity, together with his repeated nomination as "boy" or "lad," reveals him not only as the guide through nothing's realm, but as the guide to that realm where those who do not enter "as a little child shall in no wise enter therein" (Luke 18:17). The deprivation of his reason bars The Fool from the company of the wise children of this world—but it enrolls him among the children of light (Luke 16:8). In the night and cold that body forth nothingness, he accordingly offers a new pattern for the conduct of life; in convoluted irony he observes that "This cold night will turn us all to fools and madmen" (III.iv.81). And meanings come together and then re-open, as, in figures moving from concave to convex and back again, The Fool's gentle leadership in the state of cold and night is recognized. This being, below the level of the proud term *homo sapiens,* is now hailed as "sapient sir" (III.vi.24). This being, whose identity rests on the supposed absence of his judgment, is now placed beside the "robed man of justice" as a "yoke-fellow of equity" (III.vi.38–9). And if the three justices of the mad society, in their kingdom of cold and night, ludicrously catch up the figures of Rhadamanthus, Aeacus, and Minos, the dread judges of Hades, their situation also, in still more transfiguring resonance, sounds with the overtone of man's highest reach of reason toward the understanding of human society. For as Edgar, the "Noble philosopher" (III.iv.177), the "learned Theban" (III.iv.162), the "good Athenian" (III.iv.185), directs the madmen in the hovel toward the need to "deal justly" (III.vi.42), he directs attention thereby toward the Athenian philosopher who discussed, with the aristocrats assembled in the bright house of Cephalus, "this matter of doing right" (*Republic* 331C).

But in the mad dialogue of the world of nothingness, only The Fool is to the manner born. The interlocutor Lear is new-fledged in madness; the interlocutor Edgar, an impostor in madness. The utterance of all, however, is authenticated by new unfoldings of "Reason in madness" (IV.vi.179). It is, indeed, one of the marvels of this play that the language of madness does not decrease meaning, even though its syntax is dislocated from the semantic anchorages of ordinary reference; instead, and almost unbelievably, it enriches meaning to a degree that goes almost beyond analysis. In undertaking his linguistic variations Shakespeare utilized techniques supplied by a tradition recognized by both audience and actors—indeed, such virtuosities of art rarely occur except as the culmination of a tradition. We may, perhaps, identify the roots of the technique as the folk drama, for E. K. Chambers notes, in *The English Folk-Play,* that the mummer's play, in being transmitted orally, refracted into variations of formulaic language that sometimes appeared as sentences so garbled as to forfeit all meaning, but were enshrined nonetheless in the local version of the play and accepted by the folk. Such a tolerance of semantic dislocation perhaps prepared the ground for the *cadenza*-like scenes of madness in Kyd and Marlowe; and by Jacobean times the indication of madness was a familiar appurtenance of tragic drama.

But nothing like the madness of *King Lear* has ever existed, before or since. It does not merely provide an ornamental vehicle for acting virtuosity; nor does it merely set up or reinforce a dramatic mood. Again and again its language flames unexpectedly toward a re-alignment of objects and conceptions, and in doing so it creates new ideas, uncovers old ones, cuts through to new relevances. Madness, in short, is not an appendage to the tragedy, but rather an integral symbol of the humiliation of reason that constitutes the play's paradoxical educative process. The hierarchical world of *Lear* has been, in one sense, a world where normal syntax and reference have ceased to be a bond between human beings; it is at once daring and proper, therefore, that the play renews communication and meaning by the language of madness.

Now daily speech is largely a matter of decorums and predictabilities—the possibilities of word combination and reference are limited by social proprieties, by the speaker's field of sight and sound, by conventions of emphasis, by rules of sequence, and by the many other considerations that combine in the idiom of a language. The common bond of all such limiting effects is expectation, which is built up from the repetitions of daily usage. In contrast to idiomatic daily speech, language that seems mad is characterized by unpredictability of reference, and by chaos in meaning. The mad language of *Lear,* however, in still another configuration, is characterized on the one hand by unpredictability of reference, but substitutes, for chaos of meaning, an unconventional relatedness that provides special coherence.

One such form of coherence that underlies the unpredictability of *Lear*'s mad language is achieved by the insertion of reference to inexplicit background matters in place of reference to expected foreground objects or concerns. Tom-a-Bedlam's remark, "Poor Tom's a-cold" (III.iv.152), is unexpected—that is, socially unconventional—in its phrasing as in its many repetitions, but in its reference to the central and pervading fact of the cold of the hovel dwellers' situation it is not only coherent, but freshly pertinent. Again, Lear's question, "What is the cause of thunder?" (III.iv.160), is madly irrelevant to Gloucester's offer to "bring you where both fire and food is ready" (III.iv.158), but is highly pertinent to the general background fact of storm. And Edgar's identification of Gloucester, with his torch, as "the foul fiend Flibbertigibbet" (III.iv.120), takes a mad consequence from the repeated recognitions, in Tom's prior language, of the fiend's existence. Gloucester's attempt to bring Lear back to shelter is answered disjointedly by Lear's mad "First let me talk with this philosopher" (III.iv.-159). But Gloucester's sane words, though they are more expected in the context of daily situations, actually have less pertinence than Lear's mad response. For Edgar, by his commandments ("Take heed o' th' foul fiend. Obey thy parents; keep thy word justly; swear not; commit not with man's sworn spouse; set not thy sweet heart on proud array" [III.iv.82–5]) has in fact established, in the mad context of the world of storm and night, his claim as a "philosopher" more surely than Gloucester has established his as benefactor.

Again, to Lear's question, "What is your study?" Edgar's mad response, "How to prevent the fiend, and to kill vermin" (III.iv.164), accords with the background concerns of Tom-a-Bedlam's woeful existence, postulated as occurring amid vermin and the fear of the fiend ("Poor Tom, that eats the swimming frog, the toad, the tadpole, the wall-newt, and the water; that in the fury of his heart, when the foul fiend rages . . . swallows the old rat" [III.iv.134–8]). And Lear's mad statement on seeing Gloucester, "Ha! Goneril, with a white beard!" (IV.vi.97), focuses the foreground observation of

Gloucester's age with the sense of his woe, and refers them back, in madness, to the source of woe uppermost in Lear's mind: Goneril. Still another variation of the recombination of the expectations for emphasis and reference occurs in Lear's "they told me I was everything; 'tis a lie, I am not ague-proof" (IV.vi.106–7). In the normal emphasis necessary to the climactic exception for "everything," a word like "ague-proof" sounds mad; but it is enormously relevant both to Lear's prior ignorance and to the condition of cold that holds together the world of storm and night.

In general, throughout the many variations of *King Lear*'s mad usage there seem to be two constants: an unexpected reference but also a hidden propriety or similitude by which meaning is maintained. When Goneril is identified as a "joint-stool" (III.vi.55), the woodenness of the stool leads to the propriety of the word "warp'd," which refers to situations logical for wood, and also, metaphorically, to situations logical for countenances; hence the joint-stool justifies succeeding statements about Regan: "And here's another, whose warp'd looks proclaim/ What store her heart is made on" (III.-vi.56–7). The mad, and wonderful, proposal to anatomize Regan to see if there is "any cause in nature that make these hard hearts?" (III.vi.81–2) takes up the word "heart" from the prior statement; it finds "hard" hearts in common metaphorical usage; but it derives hearts that can actually have their hardness cut with a knife only from the hardness supplied by Regan's warped woodenness. The mad little sequence of reference constantly overthrows expectation of the words appropriate in normal situations, but at the same time is held together by means of the joint-stool invocation.

But the initial introduction of the joint-stool, where the situation itself indicates Goneril, is itself a psychological rather than a linguistic affect of madness—is an instance of hallucination. It is the repeated motif of hallucination—the treating of an absent object as present—expressed in the unpredictabilities and subliminal coherences in the mad pattern of language, that provides the indispensable impetus to the movement of *Lear*'s action through the realm of storm and night. For the coördinates of a more joyous possibility—justice and love—are by this means created out of the context of nothingness. In a sense both justice and love have been involved in the play's background from the very beginning; the injustice of a "third more opulent than your sisters" and its attendant denial of love have, however, made their presence a negative realization. Their creation from madness, therefore, ironically accords with the subliminal coherence that regulates the mad language of Lear. But their positive existence arises in each case from nothing—is the affirmation of an hallucinatory situation. Justice is affirmed as a need of society in the hallucinatory trial of Goneril and Regan; love, in the hallucinatory interview of Lear and Gloucester. "Dost thou know me?" asks the blinded Gloucester of the mad king. "I remember thine eyes well enough. Dost thou squiny at me? No, do thy worst, blind Cupid; I'll not love" (IV.vi.138–41). The god of love is an hallucinatory presence, but the logic of his invocation arises from the similitude of Gloucester's palpable blindness to Cupid's mythical blindness. And in especially marvelous effect, the hallucinatory negation of an imaginary command—the "I'll not love"—creates the positive reality of the command.

The same logic, in which meaning moves from word to word, from emotion to emotion, rather than in the expected forms of sequent statement, leads, in the hallucinatory interview of Gloucester and Lear, to an exponential intensification of the scope and concern of justice. "You see how this world goes," says Lear,

Glou. I see it feelingly.

Lear. What, art mad? A man may see how this world
goes with no eyes. Look with thine ears; see how
yond justice rails upon yond simple thief. Hark,
in thine ear: change places, and, handy-dandy,
which is the justice, which is the thief?

(IV.vi.151–8)

. . . The usurer hangs the cozener.
Through tatter'd clothes small vices do appear;
Robes and furr'd gowns hide all.

(IV.vi.167–9)

With this declaration, arising out of the matrix of
madness, the reductive process of divisiveness and blame
that led to the world of storm and night is reversed—
as are all the assumptions of the hierarchical world.
Though the speech is mad in its hallucinatory reference
to people not physically present, it brings to burning
focus some of the great themes and ideas that have repeatedly defined the action of the play. And it takes up
special motives—sight, clothes, the abusive tirade—that
have been freighted with the deepest kind of meaning
in the tragedy's metaphorical background and rhetorical
realization.

By such means does a renewal of spirit, emerging
from madness and nothing, lay the basis for a recreation
of the cosmos of *King Lear* and of a new reality in the
relationships of its inhabitants. The arrogant ignorance
and false knowledge of Lear at the beginning of the
play—the *docta ignorantia* by whose formula, "Nothing
will come of nothing" (I.i.92), he lost the reality of love
—is now, by means of that "use of nothing" gently
shown him by his Fool (I.iv.145), overthrown in the
wonder of the renewal of love. "Love," as Jaspers says,
and its corollary, "communication"—the latter term
implying the achievement of community as well as the
utterance of speech—are forms of becoming one's self

that appear in existence "wie eine Schöpfung aus nichts" —like a creation from nothing. "Creaturely reality," asserts Barth of the Christian truth that refutes the pagan logic of *ex nihilo nihil,* "means reality on the basis of a *creatio ex nihilo,* a creation out of nothing."

But this renewal of the spirit—this emergence from nothing of love, communication, and human concern— does not occur at a defined place and time of the play. Rather, like the glory of spring, it is suddenly apparent, not in one place, but in many places, not in one form, but in many forms. In this sweetest of the play's pluralizations, we see not merely the alleviation of an individual's travail, but the birth of the moral life of the world. "I did her wrong—" says Lear (I.v.25)—and a bud pushes into the light. "If Edgar live, O bless him!" says Gloucester (IV.vi.40)—and, in another situation, a leaf unfolds. "Let's exchange charity," says Edgar to his dying brother (V.iii.166)—and a scale falls away. Even Edmund, panting for life, pays homage to the new reality: "Some good I mean to do,/ Despite of mine own nature" (V.iii.243–4). "O Goneril!" says Albany,

> You are not worth the dust which the rude wind
> Blows in your face.
> . . . Gloucester, I live
> To thank thee for the love thou show'dst the King,
> And to revenge thine eyes.
>
> (IV.ii.29–31,95–7)

and his turning toward light has no other cause than the stirring in his heart. Yet the most symbolic trope of the new creation from nothing is the moral action of Cornwall's servant. Bred by Cornwall, fed by Cornwall, faceless in his anonymity, the servant, "thrill'd with remorse," suddenly intervenes at the bottom point between the two blindings of Gloucester: "Hold your hand, my lord!" (III.vii.72). So unexpected, so uncaused, so unpredicted, so unequivocal—the act would not have been conferred on an anonymous servant by anyone except Shakespeare; but once conferred, we see the exquisite truth of its witness. The servant's abandonment of self in concern for another spreads to his fellows like a gospel. "Let's follow the old earl, and get the Bedlam/ To lead him," says a second servant; "Go thou; I'll fetch some flax and whites of eggs/ To apply to his bleeding face," says a third (III.vii.103–4, 106–7).

In this new growth, the most wonderful plant is Lear's. Watered in one world by The Fool, in another by Cordelia, it branches outward in concern as it grows upward in conviction. In the universal fact of the coldness of the world Lear first finds the common denominator by which self-concern combines with concern for others:

> My wits begin to turn.
> Come on, my boy. How dost, my boy? Art cold?
> I am cold myself. . . .
> Poor Fool and knave, I have one part in my heart
> That's sorry yet for thee.
>
> (III.ii.68–73)

In the school of nothingness such understanding grows to action. For the first time Lear puts another before himself, and in doing so tears off the locks that have closed him in his self:

> In, boy; go first. You houseless poverty,—
> Nay, get thee in. I'll pray, and then I'll sleep.
> Poor naked wretches, whereso'er you are,
> That bide the pelting of this pitiless storm,
> How shall your houseless heads and unfed sides,
> Your loop'd and window'd raggedness, defend you
> From seasons such as these? O, I have ta'en
> Too little care of this!
>
> (III.iv.26–33)

And as courtesy grows into concern, and concern for one into concern for others, the purgation of arrogance by nothing continues. In language of madness that prophesies the lusts that have not yet been realized in the camp of Edmund and the sisters, Lear also seems to prophesy, by the terms of his by now enormously developed moral vision, a still higher elevation of possibility: "I pardon that man's life. What was thy cause?/ Adultery?/ Thou shalt not die. Die for adultery! No" (IV.vi.111–13). Though the language, still flaming, then shudders back into night and nothingness ("Let copulation thrive. . . . Down from the waist they are Centaurs,/ Though women all above. . . . Give me an ounce of civet; good apothecary, sweeten my imagination." [IV.vi.-116–33]), by its light there has been glimpsed a sublime parallel.

> Master, this woman was taken in adultery, in the very act. Now Moses in the law commanded us, that such should be stoned: but what sayest thou? . . . So when they continued asking him, he lifted up himself, and said unto them, He that is without sin among you, let him first cast a stone at her. (John 8:4–7)

With such a vision straining against his madness, Lear rises again: "None does offend, none, I say, none" (IV.-vi.172).

In his renewal of spirit Lear begins to transcend the state of his fellows in adversity, and moves toward horizons that go beyond the conception of dramatic action. Where Kent, and Gloucester, and Edgar rise out of nothing to a landing above the mockery of an Epicurean cosmos, they can climb no higher than the more noble, but no less bleak, world of the Stoics. "It is the stars,/ The stars above us, govern our conditions," says Kent in Stoic recognition of fate (IV.iii.34–5); and Edgar renders like obeisance to the Stoic ethic: "Men must endure/ Their going hence even as their coming hither;/ Ripeness is all" (V.ii.9–11). Such salutations of an inexorable order are the utterance of the Stoic "wise men"; and order, even though inexorable, stands above nothingness, as it stands above Epicurean chance. But the Stoic cannot break out of the upper limits of a cosmos that in its closedness is "cheerless, dark, and deadly" (V.iii.290).

But Lear, in language that rises above the top of the world, continues to accelerate his upward movement of love and meaning. Amid the clustered ranks of "certain philosophers of the Epicureans, and of the Stoicks" (Acts 17:18), he testifies to a "new doctrine"—speaks "strange things to our ears" (Acts 17:19–20); and he rises beyond the times and bounds of our habitation. The sealings of the cosmos are symbolically broken by Lear's recovery in the camp of Cordelia. "The great rage . . . is kill'd in him," says the doctor (IV.vii.78–9). And the doctor, echoing the doctor of the mummer's play, performs that other doctor's function: the symbolic assistance to rebirth from death—but here to a life beyond life. The renewal of consciousness from oblivion, the renewal of mind from madness, the reconciliation with a loved child lost—all these emphases transmute the reawakening of Lear to an experience of heaven. "You do me wrong," says the awakening Lear to Cordelia, "to take me out o' th' grave"—for he is in the presence of "a soul in bliss" (IV.vii.45–6). In place of the unrest of his slender self-knowledge, he now sees "a very foolish, fond old man" (IV.vii.60)—and by his true vision makes tranquil the fact of age. The scene is couched in language of divine tenderness:

> Do not laugh at me;
> For, as I am a man, I think this lady
> To be my child Cordelia.
> *Cor.*   And so I am, I am.

And the choking loveliness of her reply is tightened in still more ineffable poignance:

> I know you do not love me; for your sisters
> Have, as I do remember, done me wrong:
> You have some cause, they have not.
> *Cor.*   No cause, no cause.

The reunion gives voice to meanings more dear even than justice or communal concern—for in reconciliation and forgiveness it speaks our sweetest words:

> You must bear with me.
> Pray you now, forget and forgive;
>
> (IV.vii.68–85)

Yet the moment of transcendent peace is only a moment. Swept before the calamitous onrush of hatred and violence in the world, it seems that truly "King Lear hath lost" (V.ii.6). Cordelia and Lear are captured. Confinement and death are their only future. But the great language gathers again. Through woe following woe, Lear, breaking all shackles of event, continues the ascent of spirit. In words of triumphant life he rejects the world; he welcomes prison with the joy of paradise; he sings of happiness, of laughter, of winged creatures, of forgiveness, of blessing, of praying, of God; he pities the great ones of the earth, transient and huddled, in animal packs and mistaken sects of belief, fluid and insubstantial, moved and lighted by inauthentic stars:

> No, no, no, no! Come, let's away to prison;
> We two alone will sing like birds i' th' cage.
> When thou dost ask me blessing, I'll kneel down
> And ask of thee forgiveness. So we'll live,
> And pray, and sing, and tell old tales, and laugh
> At gilded butterflies, and hear poor rogues
> Talk of court news; and we'll talk with them too,
> Who loses and who wins, who's in, who's out;

> And take upon's the mystery of things
> As if we were God's spies; and we'll wear out,
> In a wall'd prison, packs and sects of great ones,
> That ebb and flow by th' moon.

> (V.iii.8–19)

The tropes of caged birds and gilded butterflies lift our gaze upwards. "The wing," says Plato, "is the corporeal element which is most akin to the divine" (*Phaedrus* 246D); the spirit, says John, is like a dove (John 1:32). From their golden elevation, looking out with the light of God, Lear and Cordelia, all distance of age bridged by eternity, laugh and tell the old tales that confirm the carefree happiness of beloved children; while in the world of power below the dreadful unmeaning of struggle is revealed to their bliss as an inconsequent game of in and out. And even with Cordelia dead, with reason again tottering, Lear's spirit holds fast our own. He looks on Cordelia and says, "Her voice was ever soft/ Gentle, and low; an excellent thing in woman" (V.iii.-272–3). The specification, so filled with the commonplace of daily encounters, and hence so resistant to the onceness of death, prepares for the tragedy's last wonder:

> And my poor fool is hang'd! No, no, no life!
> Why should a dog, a horse, a rat, have life,
> And thou no breath at all? Thou'lt come no more,
> Never, never, never, never, never!
> Pray you, undo this button. Thank you, sir.
> Do you see this? Look on her, look, her lips.
> Look there, look there!

> (V.iii.305–11)

Grouped around "never"—the awful hammer that pounds human duration into eternity—mourning woodwind words breathe their final variations. The Fool, who before the moment of his first appearance in the play had "much pined away" at "my young lady's going into France" (I.iv.79–80), symbolically rejoins the image and meaning of Cordelia in Lear's heart. The animal kingdom's menace to human meaning is now at last dispelled—for by love a single human existence is valued, in immeasurable worth, beyond the thought of all such grouping. The garment of the soul is once more opened —but the gentle care that undoes a single button reproves the harsh and maddened hands that earlier tore at all. The courteous "Thank you, sir" rebukes the old tirades of hatred's time. And vision, in its final thematic return, discerns, in sublime ambivalence, the flush of hope that all the ages have sought in the countenance of their dead.

Suggested Reading

Commentary on Shakespeare has proliferated enormously, and the fact constitutes both a hindrance and a deliverance for the student. Although no one can expect to exhaust this ocean—not to speak of the new streams ceaselessly fed it by busy printers—the very impossibility of doing so turns the student to a more meaningful task: he is urged to replace lengthy bibliographies with intense study of the plays themselves. Toward this end, I suggest that he make available to himself only a few aids to orientation, and read only a few discussions of each play (a controversial, or even perverse, discussion can often be as useful in calling attention to problems as one more generally praised).

The student's need for basic orientation can be divided into four areas. First of all, he should be aware of pertinent facts surrounding Shakespeare's career and activity, and for this purpose I recommend E. K. Chambers, *William Shakespeare; A Study of Facts and Problems,* 2 vols. (Oxford: Clarendon Press, 1930). Secondly, he should have some awareness of the drama of Shakespeare's predecessors and contemporaries, and for this purpose I recommend, as introduction, Thomas Marc Parrott and Robert Hamilton Ball, *A Short View of Elizabethan Drama* (New York: Charles Scribner's Sons; The Scribner Library SL 11, 1958), and as complementary one-volume anthologies of the plays themselves, *Chief Pre-Shakespearean Dramas,* ed. Joseph Quincy Adams (Cambridge, Mass.: Houghton Mifflin Co., 1924) and *Elizabethan Plays,* ed. Hazelton Spencer (Boston: D. C. Heath & Co., 1933). Thirdly, he should be aware of Shakespeare's use of sources; he might purchase Kenneth Muir's brief commentary,

Shakespeare's Sources; Comedies and Tragedies (London: Methuen & Co., 1957), and he should consult the as yet unfinished seven-volume *Narrative and Dramatic Sources of Shakespeare,* ed. Geoffrey Bullough (London: Routledge and Paul, 1957; New York: Columbia University Press, 1957). Lastly, he should have some idea of the chief historical emphases of Shakespeare criticism. *Eighteenth Century Essays on Shakespeare,* ed. David Nichol Smith, second edition (Oxford: The Clarendon Press, 1963) is indispensable, and also useful is *Shakespeare Criticism; A Selection (1623–1840),* with an introduction by David Nichol Smith (London: Oxford University Press: The World's Classics, 212, 1916–1958).

Five titles for further reading on the background of tragedy and five for each of the four plays I have treated are suggested as follows:

For the theory of tragedy:

Aristotle's Poetics, trans. S. H. Butcher, with an introduction by Francis Fergusson (New York: Hill and Wang, 1961).

Karl Jaspers, *Tragedy is Not Enough* (Boston: The Beacon Press, 1952). This work is a translated extract from Jaspers' *Von der Wahrheit.*

Henry Alonzo Myers, *Tragedy; A View of Life* (Ithaca, New York: Cornell University Press, 1956).

Friedrich Nietzsche, *The Birth of Tragedy and The Genealogy of Morals,* trans. Francis Golffing (New York: Doubleday & Co.: Anchor Books, 1956).

Miguel de Unamuno, *Tragic Sense of Life,* trans. E. Crawford Flitch (New York: Dover Publications, 1954).

For *Hamlet:*

A. C. Bradley, "Hamlet," *Shakespearean Tragedy* (Cleveland and New York: Meridian Books, 1962), pp. 109–143 [first printed 1904].

G. Ernest Jones, *Hamlet and Oedipus* (New York: W. W. Norton & Co., 1949).

L. C. Knights, *An Approach to 'Hamlet'* (Stanford: Stanford University Press, 1961).

Maynard Mack, "The World of Hamlet," *Tragic Themes in Western Literature,* ed. Cleanth Brooks (New Haven: Yale University Press: Yale Paperbound, 1960), pp. 30–58.

J. Dover Wilson, *What Happens in Hamlet* (New York: The Macmillan Co., 1935).

For *Othello:*

A. C. Bradley, "Othello," *Shakespearean Tragedy* (Cleveland and New York: Meridian Books, 1962), pp. 144–96 [first printed 1904].

Harley Granville-Barker, "Othello," *Prefaces to Shakespeare* (Princeton: Princeton University Press, 1946–7), II, 3–149 [first printed 1945].

Robert B. Heilman, *Magic in the Web; Action and Language in Othello* (Lexington: University of Kentucky Press, 1956).

G. Wilson Knight, "The *Othello* Music," *The Wheel of Fire; Interpretations of Shakespearean Tragedy* (Cleveland and New York: Meridian Books, 1962), pp. 97–119 [first printed 1930].

F. R. Leavis, "Diabolic Intellect and the Noble Hero: or The Sentimentalist's Othello," *The Common Pursuit* (London: Chatto & Windus, 1953), pp. 136–159.

For *Antony and Cleopatra:*

John F. Danby, "The Shakespearean Dialectic; An Aspect of 'Antony and Cleopatra,'" *Scrutiny,* XVI (1949), 196–213.

Harold C. Goddard, "Antony and Cleopatra," *The Meaning of Shakespeare* (Chicago: University of Chicago Press, 1951), pp. 570–594.

Harley Granville-Barker, "Antony and Cleopatra," *Prefaces to Shakespeare* (Princeton: Princeton University Press, 1946–7), I, 367–458 [first printed 1930].

Derek Traversi, "Antony and Cleopatra," *Shake-*

speare: The Roman Plays (London: Hollis & Carter, 1963), pp. 79–203.

Mark van Doren, "Antony and Cleopatra," *Shakespeare* (New York: Henry Holt & Co., 1939), pp. 267–281.

For *King Lear:*

A. C. Bradley, "King Lear," *Shakespearean Tragedy* (Cleveland and New York: Meridian Books, 1962), pp. 197–263 [first printed 1904].

John F. Danby, *Shakespeare's Doctrine of Nature; A Study of King Lear* (London: Faber and Faber, 1949).

Robert B. Heilman, *This Great Stage; Image and Structure in King Lear* (Baton Rouge: Louisiana State University Press, 1948).

G. Wilson Knight, "The *Lear* Universe," *The Wheel of Fire; Interpretations of Shakespearean Tragedy* (Cleveland and New York: Meridian Books, 1962), pp. 177–206 [first printed 1930].

Kenneth Muir, "Introduction" to *King Lear* in *The Arden Edition of The Works of William Shakespeare* (Cambridge, Mass.: Harvard University Press, 1952), pp. xv-lxiv.

Index